Preface

D1072384

This cookbook contains recipes that have been collected over decades, recipes for people who want to heal their bodies and love delicious food. Yes, healing and delicious can go hand in hand!

I tried to put this book together as if you were in the kitchen with me. In each section I have included information that I hope you will find useful on your journey toward healing and recipes that will delight everyone at your table. And why tell anyone that you are on a special diet? Instead, make and serve these delicious foods and just bask in the appreciation of your friends and family!

Be sure to read about the principles underlying the Body Ecology Way in the Introduction, starting on page 7, and then enjoy how eating well can change your life. *It's the Way to BE.*

– *Donna Gates, M.Ed, ABAAHP*

Founder, Body Ecology
Author, The Body Ecology Diet

"This book is wholeheartedly dedicated to the millions of people who are confused and frustrated because their health is suffering and they don't know where to turn."

Living Cookbook

Deliciously Healing Foods for a Happier, Healthier World

Erin Gates, project manager
Edited by Stephanie Marr
Cover photography by Jeff Skeirik
Food photography by Ideas in Food
Design/layout by JRocket77 Graphic Design

Published by Body Ecology, Inc.
www.BodyEcology.com

Table of Contents

Table of Contents

Introduction

Cooking to Heal

The Body Ecology Diet foods have the amazing power to build your immune system and to nourish both your body and your soul!

As you prepare these recipes, please do so with an intention to heal. A cook's vibrations are always in the food! In fact, in earlier times, many spiritual teachers would choose their most spiritually elevated devotees to prepare food for them, knowing that only a well-balanced, centered person with a gentle, humble soul has the power to create food with a harmonious and positive energy.

The best-kept secret to creating delicious meals is to prepare them with a heart of gratitude. When you do, the food "feels" your energy and responds in a loving way. This is the true meaning of the saying "food is medicine".

> Whether you cook for yourself or also for those you love, it's important to prepare each meal with the intention to heal, and with calmness and appreciation for the benefits that healthy, nutritious food can bring.

Masaru Emoto studied the effects that positive and negative energy have on water. His research showed that water actually responds to the energy directed toward it. When beautiful music, pictures or words of love were shown or spoken to the water, it formed beautiful crystals after it was frozen. If angry, hateful words were directed toward the water it formed ugly, distorted crystals. Because food is made largely of water it too responds to our emotions. Similarly, entering the kitchen to prepare a meal while holding the intention of love and gratitude for healthy foods, creates a meal that is that much more delicious and nourishing.

Share this value of having gratitude for nutritious healthy food with your children. Teach them to savor each bite with deep appreciation, knowing that they are truly feeding their bodies with what they need.

Research on the brain has shown that children remember habits, not our words, so start your children out with healthy ones. Create the practice of gathering around the kitchen where healthy food is being prepared and enjoyed. If you do, then that is what they will grow up remembering and hopefully one day recreate for their own children.

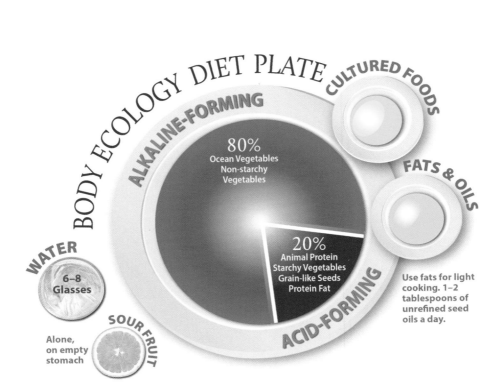

BODY ECOLOGY DIET PLATE

CULTURED FOODS

ALKALINE-FORMING

80%
Ocean Vegetables
Non-starchy
Vegetables

FATS & OILS

20%
Animal Protein
Starchy Vegetables
Grain-like Seeds
Protein Fat

ACID-FORMING

Use fats for light
cooking. 1–2
tablespoons of
unrefined seed
oils a day.

WATER

6–8
Glasses

SOUR FRUIT

Alone,
on empty
stomach

What is Body Ecology? ■ ■ ■ ■ ■ ■ ■

Body Ecology is a system of health and healing. And yes, there is a diet. Tens of thousands of people worldwide now follow the Body Ecology Way of Life to find solutions for conditions like candida, chronic fatigue, depression, weight problems, early aging, ADHD, autism, hormone imbalance, and autoimmune disorders.

As you experience the recipes in this cookbook, you too will see that they are not only healing, but are delicious as well. For decades, people have written to report that after several weeks they see a dramatic improvement in their health. Gluten-free, sugar-free, and rich in probiotic foods, Body Ecology is based on 7 universal laws or principles that help us solve much of the mystery around healing. Our initial goal is to recreate, as closely as possible, the original process that Nature uses to establish our inner ecosystem.

We are often asked what separates The Body Ecology Diet from other diets. The magic of The Body Ecology Diet starts with healing your digestive tract, where both disease and wellness begin. At least 70 percent of our immune system resides in our gut. The beneficial microbes living there help us digest our foods, strengthen our immunity so that we can conquer infections, and much more.

More than a hundred years ago, Eli Metchnikoff noted that people eating fermented foods lived longer, healthier lives. I coined the term "the inner ecosystem" to describe this internal world of beneficial microbes that should be flourishing in the intestines. This inner ecosystem is the key to health and longevity, a fact that is well validated by scientific research and is now called the "microbiome."

My fascination with the ability to heal with food began early in my life. I studied to be a dietitian in college and found it to be too one-sided—lots of science but no real focus on the wisdom of Nature. My own kitchen soon became my laboratory. And the path that I would eventually embark upon would lead me to rediscover ancient healing foods and ultimately discover the key to unlocking the body's innate intelligence to heal.

The Body Ecology Diet was originally created to help overcome candidiasis (a fungal or yeast infection); a condition that millions of people have. It soon became very clear that The Diet does so much more.

After more than 30 years of studying, and then bridging the gap between Chinese medicine and traditional Western medicine, what evolved into the Body Ecology Way is now a very effective method for addressing the root cause of disease. Most of the recipes in this book are designed for those on Stage 1 of Body Ecology and will allow anyone with candidiasis or other disorders to enjoy delicious tasting foods while healing.

Over years of experimenting and researching, Body Ecology has dispelled popular misconceptions about certain demonized foods such as coconut oil. For example, after learning from Dr. Ray Peat that coconut oil was beneficial for the thyroid, I became intrigued and wanted to uncover the real truth about this source of saturated fat from the plant kingdom. I also learned from Dr. Mary Enig, whose research at the University of Maryland had identified anti-fungal and anti-viral fatty acids in coconut oil, and I began to teach about its many benefits, especially for candidiasis and viral infections. In a few years, the use of coconut oil in our diet began to soar, especially after Bruce Fife published his excellent books. Thanks to the teamwork of a handful of coconut oil advocates working together, often not knowing of each other's efforts, this wonderful healing fat is back in our food supply once again.

In the early 90s Americans were waking up to the fact that eating sugar is harmful to the human body. Aspartame became a popular sugar-substitute, but perhaps this was jumping from the frying pan into the fire. Knowing that sugar fueled a systemic yeast infection and that people who consumed a sugar-free diet lived longer without suffering from chronic health conditions and cancer, I began looking for a safer alternative. Knowing that we humans love the sweet taste I began introducing stevia (also known as rebaudioside) to the U.S. market. For years, Body Ecology helped educate and create the market to make stevia mainstream.

Based on a deep understanding of how the digestive tract truly affects how you look, feel, and even think, eating consciously the Body Ecology Way will change your taste buds and your life forever.

The Body Ecology Diet will help:

- Create more energy and help you age well.
- Strengthen your organs, digestive tract, and immune system.
- Conquer infections in your body.
- Cleanse your body of dangerous toxins.
- Balance your cellular biochemistry.
- Re-establish and nourish your inner ecosystem.

Emphasizing Probiotic Foods ■ ■ ■ ■ ■ ■ ■

The new stars of a truly healthy diet are fermented foods! They are the missing link in all other systems of health and healing and have set Body Ecology apart from other diets for two decades. Probiotics are living microorganisms that are essential for a happy, healthy life. Probiotic means "for life" and the right probiotic foods are full of friendly bacteria and yeast, and are essential for wellness.

Probiotic foods have amazing attributes. They can:

- Help white blood cells fight disease.
- Control putrefactive bacteria in the intestines.
- Provide important nutrients for building the blood.
- Assist digestion.
- Protect the intestinal mucosa.
- Prevent diarrhea, constipation, and contribute to bowel elimination.
- Manufacture important B vitamins and are the most abundant source of Vitamin B-12.

Body Ecology-approved fermented foods fight yeast and other unhealthy pathogens in your digestive tract. In addition to probiotics, which provide your body with beneficial microbiota (bifidus, acidophilus, beneficial yeast), these superfoods will be an important factor in recolonizing your inner microbial world.

We have been teaching people how to ferment vegetables, coconut water, and the soft spoon meat in young Thai coconuts for years. We offer probiotics in a non-dairy liquid form that contain naturally occurring microbes cultured from grain-like seeds, rice, and chickpeas. We provide you with potent protein powders made with fermented spirulina, other fermented algae, fermented cruciferous and dark green vegetables and ocean veggies. And in Stage 2, once your intestinal lining has healed, and only if dairy is right for your unique body, we teach you how to make delicious milk kefir from goat or cow milk (page 182).

The 7 Universal Principles of Body Ecology ■ ■ ■ ■ ■ ■

Body Ecology's 7 Universal Principles are guidelines for eating and healing. These are universal principles or laws that all of Nature and all humans must obey. Together they weave a system that flawlessly supports health and longevity. Used correctly, they allow us to increase our vitality and well being for years to come.

The Principle of Uniqueness: Knowing Yourself

The first of the 7 Universal Principles, the Principle of Uniqueness, states that you are a singular, one-of-a-kind individual. Yes, we have most of the same pieces and parts: a heart that beats, lungs that breathe, and a brain that thinks. But we also have diverging needs, childhood experiences, habits, and ways of thinking, learning, and being. These differences give us identity and individuality. Your uniqueness will bring its own properties to the Body Ecology program; and the Body Ecology Way is flexible, so it can be altered somewhat to meet your special needs.

The journey begins with honest self-evaluation: where are you, right now, today; and how prepared are you to embark on this new program? The first step is to get a clear snapshot of your current health status. By visiting your holistically oriented doctor (one trained in functional medicine), you can obtain helpful tests, such as a hormone panel and a genetic profile, and check the status of your minerals, fatty acids, and amino acids. You can find out what heavy metals are in your body and even determine your biological age (versus your chronological age), all of which will help clarify your individual needs and help you plan the meals that will truly nourish your own unique body.

The Principle of Step by Step: Knowing Where and How to Begin

The Principle of Step by Step is the universal law that tells us that we can't do everything we would like to do or need to do all at once. If we try, we will surely fail. Learning and change do not happen overnight. We must face take them step by step. We have many tools for healing. But please, don't try to pick up all of them right away. You can't. Take a minute to tune in to your intuition, and notice which steps feel most urgent and appealing. Try those first. Master one or two, and then add another when you are ready to do so.

You have most likely heard the expression that "a journey of a thousand miles begins with the first step." This principle tells us where to begin and what steps to take first. Anytime you are starting something new, it can feel overwhelming; however, you'll do yourself a favor by taking things step by step at a pace that feels comfortable for you. Small steps over time add up to big results. Address and follow these four simple actions to make you successful in healing:

1. **Create energy.** First and foremost, create energy. Nothing else can happen until this initial step has been taken. Evaluate your energy and take a few moments to consider the things that are draining you of vital energy: Not enough sleep? Too many commitments? Toxic relationships? The amazing superfoods and anti-aging therapies found in the Body Ecology Way provide excellent solutions to begin renewing your energy day after day…step by step.

2. **Conquer or control infections.** The Body Ecology system of health and healing, with its amazing Diet, originally began as a way to conquer yeast infections. It is the most complete and comprehensive antifungal diet available and a leader in using fermented foods and nutrition for healing.

   Today, eight out of ten Americans suffer from candidiasis. The drugs, alcohol, stress, and sweet foods so available to us have accelerated this widespread yeast/fungal problem. The lifestyles we lead give fungi even more opportunity to thrive. Infections cause inflammation. Diagnosing and conquering all infections is essential to the journey to wellness.

   Other common infections most of us are struggling with include viral herpes, bacterial infections in the gums, low-grade, chronic bacterial infections in the bladder, and H. pylori bacterial infections in the stomach.

   When infections like candida are corrected by using the Body Ecology approach, energy automatically goes up and susceptibility to disease goes down. Once infections are brought under control by your immune system, the energy to rejuvenate becomes yours.

3. **Correct digestion.** When the digestive tract doesn't work well, nothing works well. Are you experiencing some of the signs of a compromised digestive tract, such as constipation, diarrhea, inflammation in the gut, irritable bowel syndrome, and flatulence? It is essential that you heal your gut lining and establish a healthy inner

ecosystem, thus repopulating the intestinal tract with friendly microbiota.

The other part of Step-by-Step says that all of this cannot be done at once. Body Ecology has an excellent understanding of gut health and provides us with valuable tools for having a healthy digestive tract throughout life. When first starting The Diet, during the first five to ten days, many people with an inflamed mucosal lining will want to "rest" the gut by eating primarily soft or liquid foods—broths, purees, and green smoothies—and also lightly steamed leafy-green and ocean vegetables.

We encourage people to look at the many tools we have. Pick one to start. Become comfortable with it. Pick up another one and keep on going. One day you'll look back and you'll have an array of amazing tools that will serve you very well.

4. **Cleanse out toxins.** We must actively remove the toxins from our bodies. These toxins are in our organs and in our cells. They come to us from nutritionally deficient, poorly digested, and poorly combined foods. They are in the water, in the air, and even in our self-destructive feelings. They are in drug residues and ingested metals, such as lead, aluminum, and cadmium. We have inherited toxins from our parents, and we pass them on to our own children. Toxins snuff out our spiritual power and our intuition. When they are removed from our lives, boundless energy is created. Doing so is also essential for young men and women who are considering pregnancy and want to have beautiful, healthy children.

Taking a step-by-step approach to healing doesn't mean that your progress has to be slow. You can choose how quickly you embrace the steps, and you may experience immediate improvements in energy and vitality. On the other hand, you might need to go at a more moderate pace. Be realistic. Don't take on more than you can handle. When you feel comfortable with one step, move on to another.

Here are four simple steps you can take in the beginning:

1. **Cut back on or eliminate sugar and high-carb sweets.** On The Body Ecology Diet, you will be introduced to several alternative sweeteners that will allow you to still enjoy the sweet taste without the damaging effects of sugars (even honey and the "healthy" sugars).

2. **Change the oils you are currently eating to the extra-virgin, unrefined fats and oils of The Diet.** The recipes in this book will provide you with a delicious array of fats and oils to keep you looking and feeling great. They also make eating more pleasurable.

3. **Add fermented foods and probiotic liquids to your meals, such as fermented vegetables and young coconut kefir.** *This is perhaps the most important step of all,* as you'll soon learn.

4. **Pay attention to cleansing your colon.** You might consider trying your first colonic if you've never had one before. Cells must eliminate their toxic waste. When you're constipated, so are your cells. They, too, feel toxic, sluggish, and irritable. Actively cleansing with diet, herbs, colonics, and home enemas will soon become commonplace as more of us begin to understand that we must assist our body in its attempt to purify.

Success comes step by step. That's why you must be very determined to stick with The Diet until you master it. Advance according to your own personal pace, but persevere. As you begin to implement The Diet, I hope you will treat your body as an evolving experiment in self-awareness. Unlike other dietary approaches, the Body Ecology Way is not a short-term "fix," but rather an ongoing journey of personal discovery and adaptation.

The Principle of Cleansing: Purify from the Inside Out

Nature is always cleansing herself with wind, rain, heat, and cold. Cleansing is Nature's way of allowing the body to get rid of unwanted toxins, waste, and foreign substances, playing a vital role in preventing disease.

If we are to enjoy optimum health, toxins must come out of the cells in our organs. Cleansing is the process that accomplishes this by carrying away cellular debris.

What most of us don't realize is that our bodies are constantly working on our behalf to purify and cleanse us of these toxins. A speck of dust gets in your eye, and you blink and tear up to cleanse out the dust to wash it away so it won't hurt you. A similar thing happens when a virus invades your system and you get a fever; it's your immune system working to purify your body of that toxin. In fact, the ability to purge toxins out of each cell is really quite remarkable. (We pay extra for ovens that are self-cleaning, yet our bodies do it for us for free!)

On The Body Ecology Diet, cell walls remain soft and pliable from antioxidant-rich plant foods. Nutrients carried in your bloodstream enter your cells, while waste products are sent back out into the bloodstream, where they are eliminated in a variety of ways. Examples of how the body eliminates toxins are: bowel movements, urination, skin eruptions, sweating from a fever or the summer heat, tears, vomiting, coughing up mucus, and menstruation.

Unfortunately, we have been taught that these bodily cleansings are "bad" and need to be suppressed, so we pop a few pills, keep on working, and try to pretend they're not really happening to us. Indeed, while we were growing up, we were brainwashed to stop the cleansing. Instead, we should be helping our bodies cleanse with diet, herbs, home enemas, colonic therapy, saunas, and chelation.

As you better understand the Principle of Cleansing, you will feel both the gratitude and joy that comes with realizing that our bodies were created with this amazing function embedded within us—this ability to purify in order to heal.

The Principle of Balance: The Dance of Yin and Yang

The Principle of Balance focuses on the balance between yin and yang, or contractive and expansive energies, respectively. Yin and yang are complementary opposites within The 7 Universal Principles of Body Ecology—two interdependent and creative forces of change that are always seeking equilibrium.

Yang energy is outward, activating, drying, and warm or hot. It may stimulate thoughts of the sun and of fire. Yin energy is inward, stored energy. It is nourishing, moistening, cooling, and anti-inflammatory. It may remind you of water or of the moon.

Since illness and disease are caused by imbalances, we must pay close attention to whether yin or yang dominates in the body. Yang illness emerges when there is too much fire energy (inflammation) or when we are too stressed-out (tense, with pulses racing). Yin illness occurs when we are too depleted (fragile, exhausted, and anxious).

The right foods and supplements help us build the foundation to promote lasting ideal health. And eating the right foods helps us balance, rejuvenate, and store energy.

Your Weight

Proper food combining automatically results in some weight loss because you'll no longer be bloated with the toxins that come from poor digestion. Some people can easily lose up to 10 pounds during the first two weeks after they start The Diet. This is all very normal—don't worry if you lose more weight than you want. You can reach your ideal weight once your body is back in balance and building healthy tissue. If you're already thin, you will still lose some bloating; the scales may stay the same, but you'll look different.

You also may feel hungrier than usual; again because you'll have no "bloated" or full feeling after meals. Just eat smaller amounts more often! As long as your food is properly combined, you can eat as much as you need to sustain your energy levels and not worry about gaining weight. It's fine to have four to five smaller meals throughout the day. Just allow time for a protein meal to digest (three to four hours) before switching to a meal with grain-like seeds or starchy vegetables. Vegetarian meals usually do not take as long to digest as protein meals, but the use of digestive enzymes is highly recommended.

Acid/Alkaline Foods

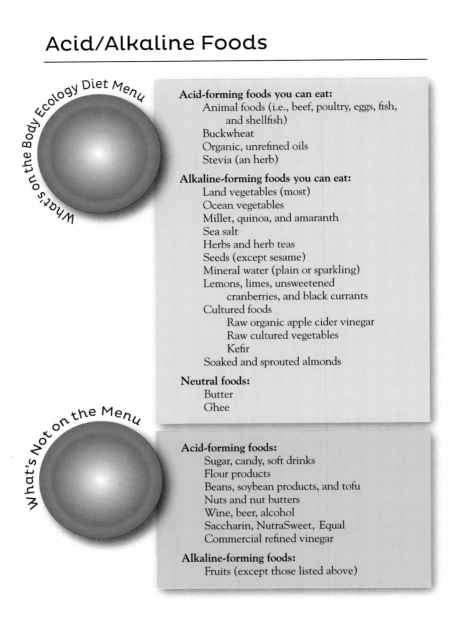

What's on the Body Ecology Diet Menu

Acid-forming foods you can eat:
Animal foods (i.e., beef, poultry, eggs, fish, and shellfish)
Buckwheat
Organic, unrefined oils
Stevia (an herb)

Alkaline-forming foods you can eat:
Land vegetables (most)
Ocean vegetables
Millet, quinoa, and amaranth
Sea salt
Herbs and herb teas
Seeds (except sesame)
Mineral water (plain or sparkling)
Lemons, limes, unsweetened cranberries, and black currants
Cultured foods
　　Raw organic apple cider vinegar
　　Raw cultured vegetables
　　Kefir
Soaked and sprouted almonds

Neutral foods:
Butter
Ghee

What's Not on the Menu

Acid-forming foods:
Sugar, candy, soft drinks
Flour products
Beans, soybean products, and tofu
Nuts and nut butters
Wine, beer, alcohol
Saccharin, NutraSweet, Equal
Commercial refined vinegar

Alkaline-forming foods:
Fruits (except those listed above)

The Principle of Acid and Alkaline: How to Choose Your Foods

One of the most amazing features of the human body is its ability to keep its internal state relatively constant. The pH—or balance between acid and alkaline—of our blood, saliva, and urine is carefully regulated within a narrow range. The ideal pH of blood should be 7.36 to 7.44; if it drops below 7.2, it has become dangerously acidic and we can die. Even a slightly acidic decline in pH allows infections, disease, and even cancer to develop inside us. It's vital that we choose foods that help to maintain our blood pH close to the ideal of 7.4.

To keep your body more alkaline, your diet should primarily consist of foods from the plant kingdom, especially vegetables from the land and the sea. The more color, the better: dark green, leafy vegetables and dark—even black—ocean veggies, properly prepared so that you can digest them, are excellent examples of alkaline foods that keep your body within that ideal pH range.

Eighty percent of your food intake should be these colorful, alkaline-forming foods, and our recipes are designed to keep your body in perfect balance.

The Principle of Food Combining and The Principle of 80/20: Go-To Guidelines for Reviving Digestion

The last two principles—Food Combining and 80/20—both have to do with optimizing your digestion. Many diseases begin with poor digestion. Fortunately for us, these two principles, along with fermented foods, take the burden of having to work so hard to digest your meals off of your digestive tract.

Food combining means to deliberately eat certain foods with other foods. We do this because when foods digest easily together, it allows the stomach, small intestine, and colon to do their jobs more efficiently. As a result, nutrients are more accessible. There is less bloating and gas in your digestive tract, and also less inflammation. Incompatible foods that do not digest properly can ferment and cause an overproduction of sugars, indigestion, and constipation. This also creates more toxins and more acidity in your body.

Food combining often seems complicated to people, but it is actually one of the easiest of the principles to implement. In fact, if you practice it for one week, it will become second nature to you. There are six simple rules to food combining:

Rule 1. Eat animal protein with non-starchy vegetables.

Rule 2. Eat grains and grain-like seeds (that is, quinoa, millet, buckwheat, and amaranth) with starchy and non-starchy vegetables.

Rule 3. Eat fruit alone, and at least 30 minutes before any other meal, or combine with a protein/fat (see Rule 5). Or combine acidic fruit with leafy-green salads.

Rule 4. Combine fats and oils with animal protein, grains, grain-like seeds, or starchy or non-starchy vegetables. Basically, oils and fats go with everything!

Rule 5. Combine protein/fats with other protein/fats. (Protein/fats are foods that contain both protein and fat, such as avocados, dairy foods, and nuts and seeds.)

Rule 6. Combine protein/starches with non-starchy vegetables from the land and ocean. (Protein/starches, such as beans, contain mostly starch but also a small amount of protein.)

80%/20% Rule #1

Stop Eating When You Are Full

80%

Leave Empty for Digestion

20%

20%

80%

Don't
"TOP OFF"
Your Tummy

While these basic rules will get you started, there is much more to learn about food combining. If you are interested in expanding your understanding, this principle is covered at length in our book *The Body Ecology Diet.*

The Principle of 80/20 works well in conjunction with that of Principle of Food Combining, as both are about correcting and improving digestion. Many of us have "eyes that are bigger than our stomachs." We eat huge portions, consuming not only to the point of satiation, but usually well beyond that. This puts far too much stress on our already overtaxed digestive tracts. The 80/20 Principle prevents this issue with three simple rules:

Rule 1. Eat until your stomach is 80 percent full, leaving 20 percent available for digestion. This means leaving the table before your stomach is full. You can always come back and eat more later!

Rule 2. Eighty percent of the food on your plate should be land and/or ocean vegetables, with the remaining 20 percent reserved for a meat protein, a grain, or starchy vegetables. Vegetables are the staple of the Body Ecology Way. Fill 80 percent your plate with non-starchy varieties, and with this alkalizing, high-fiber diet, you'll live a longer, healthier life.

Rule 3. Approximately 80 percent of the foods on your plate should be alkaline-forming, and 20 percent should be acid-forming. This rule counteracts the American tendency to eat a preponderance of acid-forming foods—animal proteins, breads, cereals, pasta, and starchy vegetables. Non-starchy vegetables are key to creating an alkaline environment in your body. A body that remains more alkaline retains more minerals—key nutrients for beauty as well as longevity.

You can read much more about the 80/20 Principle—and all of the principles outlined here—in *The Body Ecology Diet.* But for now, this baseline understanding of the principles will allow you to understand how to eat and live the Body Ecology Way: healing from the inside out.

The 2 Stages of The Body Ecology Diet

If you've come to The Diet because you have health problems, or you simply want to look and feel better, or if you've heard that's it a good diet for age management, ideally you should begin with Stage 1. At a certain point, you may want to expand your food choices and begin eating a few foods suggested for Stage 2, knowing that you can always go back to Stage 1 when you need to; however, most of the recipes in this book are Stage 1 recipes, unless otherwise noted. Stage 1 is an excellent way to eat for the rest of your life and Stage 1 foods are absolutely delicious!

On Stage 1 of The Diet, your goal is to restore your inner ecosystem, conquer your yeast infection, create more energy and better support your body in the life-long process of cleansing. Food can become your most important ally or it can be your worst enemy. That's why, in this initial stage of healing or rejuvenation, certain foods (like sugars, casein, gluten, and bad fats) must be totally avoided because they sabotage your efforts.

When any challenges you are facing have disappeared and when you've established a hearty inner ecosystem in your intestines from eating fermented foods and drinking probiotic liquids, you may be ready to start slowly introducing other foods back into your diet (Stage 2), but it's vitally important to choose only the healthiest ones.

Sadly, we've often seen people who were all too eager to begin Stage 2 get into trouble by drifting back into their old way of eating. Some were feeling sorry for themselves because they were deprived of their favorite "forbidden foods"—the ones that either made them sick in the first place or simply aggravated their symptoms. Far too many people misinterpret Stage 2 and widen their menu too quickly and/or return to eating foods that are addictive (with gluten and sugars). After falling off The Diet their symptoms reappear and they become frustrated and disappointed in themselves. If this happens to you, don't be discouraged. Just remember how much better you felt eating the nourishing and appetizing foods in Stage 1. People usually return with stronger resolve and conviction to make the best lifestyle choice. Each time that we make a conscious choice to go back to a healthier way of eating, it becomes easier to do. It feels good too—knowing we are choosing what's best for us. Remember that it takes courage, determination, and willpower to be successful at anything you do.

Are You Ready for Stage 2?

Usually after three to six months of strictly following Stage 1 of The Diet (which includes eating the fermented foods), you are ready to move cautiously into Stage 2. By now your symptoms should be gone and your energy and your overall sense of wellbeing should be back.

In Stage 2, you're still following the 7 Body Ecology Principles and enjoying the many vegetables, the healthy proteins, the grain-like seeds, and the unrefined fats and oils on Stage 1 of The Diet, but you're now ready to broaden your menu a bit. Consider slowly introducing gluten-free grains such as rice and whole oats, perhaps legumes, such as lentils, and also the sweeter vegetables you may have avoided, such as sweet potatoes and yams. (These sweeter vegetables should always be eaten with cultured vegetables and probiotic liquids so that the beneficial bacteria will consume the natural plant sugars). In Stage 2 some people can begin to introduce fermented dairy made with goat, sheep or cow milk into their diets, but many people are better off avoiding dairy completely. (See more on dairy below.)

We'd like to make it very clear that Stage 2 does not mean going back to candy bars, pasta, bread, and foods made with sugar, gluten, and refined oils. Usually if you do go back to these foods after eating a very cleansing diet like The Body Ecology Diet, your body will send a loud, clear signal that it doesn't want them anymore. If you do fall off The Diet for a short time, especially during the holidays or times when you are traveling, it doesn't take long to feel the difference.

Grains Can Be Good—Adding Them Back In

Anti-carb diets like the Atkins and Paleo diets would have you avoid grains forever. And for you that may be best. But many people find that adding certain whole, slow-burning grains back into their diet helps reduce anxiety. They also sleep better. That's because complex, slow-release carbs are rich in B vitamins and minerals that have a calming effect on the nervous system. They create energy for many of us—not only by helping us sleep better at night—but by also providing energy to the thyroid and the adrenals.

Complex, slow-burning carbs should not be put in the same category as simple sugars, such as sweet fruits, dried fruits or refined carbs (doughnuts, sandwiches, and pasta.) Slow-burning grains and grain-like seeds both help create a happier, healthier gut. They feed friendly microbiota. They provide fiber that helps hold moisture in the stool and provide the bulk needed for proper peristalsis and elimination. If you've been on a strict Paleo (high protein, high fat diet) and are not sleeping well at night, you might try eating a slow-release grain during your evening meal and see if you aren't sleeping better in a few days.

You'll always want to avoid the most reactive grains that have gluten—wheat, kamut, rye, barley and spelt. Also avoid flour products, which are gummy, glue-like foods. Try sprouted GABA rice (from TruRoots™) and gluten-free whole-oat groats. Avoid oatmeal or steel cut oats, which have not been cleaned properly before cutting and shredding. In other words, eat your newly added grains in their whole form. If you enjoy legumes, like lentils, adzuki beans and chickpeas introduce them slowly and prepare them properly. When eating these new foods you'll still want to follow the 80/20 rule. Only 20 percent of your plate should be the new grain or new bean and the remaining 80 percent should be those starchy or non-starchy vegetables or ocean vegetables that you know work well in your unique body.

Always adding a few spoonsful of cultured vegetables to your plate or drinking several ounces of a probiotic liquid will allow you to safely enjoy these complex carbs. The beneficial microbiota in the fermented foods will dine on the sugars in the grains and will also help you digest them.

For decades, nutritionists have considered legumes an excellent source of vegetarian protein; however, this is questionable because they are mostly starch and contain very little protein. They are difficult to digest. If you love beans and want to add them back into your diet, preparing them properly will make them more digestible, more balanced and more nutritious. *(See the sidebar.)*

Preparing Legumes

Like grains, legumes must be soaked for at least 8 hours to remove the phytic acid, a plant poison or anti-nutrient that inhibits digestion. When you cook legumes, boil them vigorously for 15 minutes to remove the lectins, another plant toxin that makes some people sensitive to grains and legumes. After 15 minutes of boiling, drain the beans then put them back into the stockpot and cover with filtered water. Cook them slowly with a strip of kombu, a sea vegetable, until they are tender. The kombu adds iodine as well as other alkaline minerals to the legumes, which are naturally acidic. Celtic sea salt, also alkalizing, can be added in the final 30 minutes of cooking once the beans are soft.

Because grains and beans will be new foods for your intestinal microbes they'll need a bit of time to figure out how to process them. Gas and bloating may be the result at first. Following the 80/20 rule and combining them with non-starchy vegetables (not with rice or tortillas) and eating them with cultured vegetables will reduce the gas and bloating.

What About Dairy?

Some people never do well on dairy. You will often hear me say that all foods have both a positive and a negative side to them. While fermented dairy products—like milk kefir and whey protein concentrate—help build muscles, milk is also dehydrating and mucous forming. Many people report that adding fermented kefir to their diet helps with elimination, while others tell us it makes them constipated. It's the perfect example of the Principle of Uniqueness. Everyone needs to find those special foods that work for their exceptional, one-of-a-kind body. One important tip for introducing dairy to your diet, follow the Principle of Step by Step and introduce it slowly in small amounts.

Milk kefir should be introduced into the diet only after the gut lining is healthy and a robust and diverse inner ecosystem is in place. In other words, never drink it if you have a leaky, inflamed gut lining.

Fermenting milk into milk kefir makes it more digestible since the proteins and fats are broken down and the sugars consumed by the bacteria and yeast.

Since milk is dehydrating and can cause constipation, diluting the milk with a liquid can make it less constipating. Try adding ¼ cup of milk kefir to 6 ounces of sparkling mineral water then add some fresh lemon juice and a few drops of stevia liquid concentrate. Add a spoonful of milk kefir to your favorite herbal tea or add ¼ cup to your morning smoothie. The small amount will allow the microbiome in your gut to learn how to deal with this new food.

Milk kefir is a protein/fat so it combines best with other protein fats (avocado, nuts and seeds) and with acid fruits (berries, kiwis, etc.). You may find that a little bit of raw sheep or goat cheese sprinkled on top of your raw veggie salad with some soaked and sliced almonds and/or avocado works well for you. Or another great idea for those who do well on a little bit of dairy is to make a delicious kefir salad dressing.

While Stage 2 allows more foods than Stage 1, remember that throughout life your body will be in a constant state of flux because life is filled with change. The seasons of the year, the process of aging, stress, and your emotions and beliefs will tip you into and out of balance. Your body is the only body you will ever have and it will always need your tender loving care. Begin with Stage 1, stay there forever if you'd like, or move into Stage 2 when you are ready. Be mindful and watch how your unique body responds to certain foods eating only those that make you feel stronger.

The Body Ecology Way acts as a roadmap for your healing journey. We hope that its unique diet, the delicious meals, and its 7 Principles provide the health and healing you've been seeking.

Smoothies ■ ■ ■ ■ ■ ■ ■

Green smoothies are the perfect way to replenish your body in the morning. Their mega-nutrition can energize you, balance your mood, and rehydrate after hours spent sleeping, sweating and breathing during the night. Green smoothies also alkalize your blood, which prevents disease. What's even better? A green smoothie's vitamins and minerals are quickly absorbed by the body, leaving you feeling fulfilled, clear minded, and after a while—happier! That's right, happier! Greens are very expansive, which means they allow your body to relax.

Beware of green smoothie recipes that use vegetables from the cruciferous family, especially kale. Cruciferous vegetables need to be cooked until tender, or fermented to make them more digestible and are not advised if you have a thyroid problem.

An expansive green smoothie can be balanced by adding a pinch of mineral-rich Selina Naturally's Makai or Celtic Sea Salt, which is contracting in nature. Read more about Body Ecology's Principle of Balance, and be sure to balance your meals throughout the day.

High quality, mineral rich sea salt helps produce stomach acid (hydrochloric acid (HCl)) that is essential for digestion. But also, very importantly, fruits and vegetables naturally have eggs, larva and parasites on them that we cannot see. Yes, even organic fruits and veggies do. HCl not only helps us digest protein by stimulating production of pepsin in the stomach, it is there to kill any parasites as well.

We strongly suggest that you spray or soak (for two minutes) your fruits and vegetables in a special "wash" before using them in your smoothie or any other raw recipe, including salads. Commercially made veggie washes are available online or in many health food stores. You can make your own by simply adding apple cider vinegar and lemon juice to water. Store your homemade wash in a spray bottle.

Investing in a powerful blender like a VitaMix™ or a BlendTec™ is well worth the money. They last for decades.

Smoothies for breakfast are most beneficial. We suggest you make a larger portion and drink it throughout the morning. Store any remainder in a glass container and drink it the following day. If you haven't had one yet, the warm weather marks the best time to try these healthy smoothies. You'll love the way you feel after drinking one. Play with the ingredients and create your own favorites. Just be careful not to make them too sweet.

Market Green Smoothie

■ ■ □ ■ ■ ■ ■

Ingredients:

3 organic unpeeled cucumbers, chopped

1 cup celery root, peeled, chopped

1 lemon, peeled and cut into sections

1 lime, peeled and cut into sections

1 whole organic green apple, chopped

2 inches ginger, peeled and chopped

1 heaping handful baby spinach

Filtered water to cover

1 cup of ice

Optional ingredients: frozen berries, fermented coconut meat, cultured quinoa milk, coconut kefir, and stevia to taste.

Directions:

Purée ingredients in a blender adding more water if needed.

Green apples are a sour fruit that adds a touch of sweetness to an alkaline, vegetable-rich smoothie. Ideally fruit should be eaten alone and on an empty stomach for optimum digestion, but work just fine for most people when combined with veggies. If you find that the addition of the apple is too sweet for you, then don't put it in. In other words, temporarily eliminate the apple if you are dealing with severe candida-related problems and use some fermented coconut meat and stevia to thicken and flavor your smoothie.

Good Morning Greens Smoothie

■ ■ □ ■ ■ ■ ■

Ingredients:

1 unpeeled Granny Smith apple, cored, coarsely chopped

4 or 5 celery stalks, chopped

3 to 4 large romaine lettuce leaves, torn into pieces

½ large Haas avocado, peeled and coarsely chopped

½ bunch cilantro or parsley (depending on your preference), large stems removed

3 to 4 cups filtered water

Directions:

Purée ingredients in a blender, adding more water if needed.

You can also add the juice from one half of a lemon or lime and even ¼ teaspoon sea salt and/or cayenne pepper.

Omega 3 Nutrient Boost Smoothie ■ ■ ■ ■ ■ ■ ■

Ingredients:

5 cups filtered water

1 cucumber, chopped

2 medium green zucchinis, chopped

3 stalks celery, chopped

5 stalks fresh mint

2 lemons, juiced

7 large romaine lettuce leaves, torn into pieces

3 tablespoons Barlean's Total Omega Swirl™
   (orange cream flavor)

Stevia to taste

Directions:

Purée ingredients in a blender, adding more water if needed.

Coconut Milk ■ ■ ■ ■ ■ ■ ■

Ingredients:

1 cup fresh or frozen young coconut meat

3½ cups coconut water

If you can't find young coconut meat locally, it is available from exoticsuperfoods.com.

Directions:

1. Combine young coconut meat and coconut water in a blender and process until smooth.

2. Strain through a cheesecloth, fine sieve or nut-milk bag.

Body Ecology Diet "Acidophilus Milk" ■ ■ ■ ■ ■ ■ ■

Ingredients:

1 cup filtered water

1 to 3 drops Body Ecology's stevia liquid
   concentrate, or to taste

1 tablespoon probiotic powder, such as
   Life Start by Natren (dairy-based)

1 teaspoon vanilla extract, alcohol-free

1 teaspoon lecithin granules, optional

Directions:

Purée all ingredients in a blender or shake in a jar.

Many mothers find that their very young children enjoy this "milk" in a bottle. It's a good way to make sure your baby is getting plenty of friendly microflora, and it satisfies the desire for sugar. It is not a substitute for breast milk or formula; however, it can be added to formula.

Since dairy combines with acidic fruits, there is no problem drinking this "milk" and then eating a grapefruit or drinking lemon and water.

Cultured Quinoa Milk

Ingredients:

2 cups raw quinoa

1 quart filtered water

Pinch sea salt

¼ cup young coconut kefir or 1 packet of kefir starter

Vanilla, stevia, or organic mesquite powder (optional)

Directions:

1. Soak quinoa overnight at room temperature in quart-sized covered glass container with a pinch of sea salt. Don't refrigerate.

2. Rinse and drain quinoa and put in blender. Add filtered water. Blend until very creamy. The quinoa milk will turn white.

3. Drain quinoa pulp by using a nut-milk bag (found at natural grocers) or a fine-mesh strainer. (The quinoa pulp can be fermented or cooked and used in other recipes such as soups, croquettes, loaves, baby food, pet food, etc.)

4. Pour strained quinoa milk into a sterile glass jar. Add ¼ cup young coconut kefir or 1 packet of kefir starter and seal jar.

5. Set out to ferment at 72 to 76 degrees for 18 to 24 hours, and refrigerate until ready to use.

6. Drink as-is or add sweetener or flavors listed above

Add this "milk" to smoothies for a flavor and texture almost like yogurt. You can also add it to raw soups.

Did you know that quinoa is a seed? You can also make this recipe using other seeds or nuts.

Have you seen all of the commercial fermented products on the market now? It can be very hard to determine which of these are healthy and which ones are simply trendy treats. Most store-bought fermented beverages are pasteurized and loaded with sugars and preservatives and do not contain living probiotics and enzymes. We like this delicious, more cost effective living alternative. And we think it tastes better too!

Light, Fresh, and Lovely Green Smoothie

Ingredients:

2 to 3 stalks celery, chopped

1 large zucchini, chopped

1 large cucumber, peeled, chopped

3 large romaine lettuce leaves, chopped

1 large green apple, cored, chopped

2-inch piece of ginger, peeled

1 handful fresh mint leaves, or to taste

¼ cup fresh coconut meat (optional)

3 drops of Body Ecology's liquid stevia concentrate

Directions:

Blend all ingredients together until smooth and creamy.

Cheery Cherry Smoothie

Ingredients:

1 cucumber, chopped

2 zucchinis, chopped

3 large romaine lettuce leaves, torn into pieces

¼ cup mint, leaves only

½ cup coconut meat

6 ounces (½ bag) of dark frozen cherries

12 drops stevia or to taste

1 cup Innergy Biotic or sparkling mineral water

1 cup filtered water

Directions:

Purée ingredients in a blender, adding more water if needed.

As a bonus, Cheery Cherry Smoothies are low in oxalates!

Pineapple Ginger Smoothie

Ingredients:

1 cup celeriac, chopped

1 green apple, chopped

1-inch piece ginger, chopped

2 large zucchinis, chopped

1 16-ounce package frozen pineapple

2 tablespoons coconut butter

1 cup Innergy Biotic

4 cups filtered water

Directions:

Purée ingredients in a blender, adding more water if needed.

Notes

Notes

Brunch or Lunch ■ ■ ■ ■ ■

When planning a delicious Sunday brunch, eggs are a natural. Eggs help strengthen the thyroid, which is often weak in people with candidiasis. Because they are such a concentrated, contracting food, most of us will find that eating them midday is best. Your body will then have plenty of time and energy to digest them. At breakfast, when you're trying to make your body more open or expanded, they may be too contracting. Still, their strongly contracting nature creates energy useful for those with very active mornings. If you sit at a desk during the day, eat them for lunch or dinner.

One beneficial way to prepare eggs is over easy (a soft, runny yolk) in organic coconut oil or ghee. Then, mostly eat the yolk. The cooked egg white (protein) is difficult to digest. Contrary to popular belief, it is the egg yolk that contains the most important nutrients in the egg, such as DHA and Vitamins A and D.

Eggs are sorely misunderstood these days. Yes, they do have cholesterol, but they are comparatively low in fat. The yolk also contains lecithin, which aids in fat assimilation. Eggs actively raise the level of HDL, which is the good cholesterol, and they have the most perfect protein components of any food. Today, even though we Americans have drastically cut our egg consumption, there has not been a decline in heart disease. If you have been an egg lover and have given them up, you can now enjoy them by eating them appropriately. Remember to combine them with lots of alkaline vegetables to balance their acidic nature. Raw cultured vegetables are an excellent expansive food that balances the contracting power of eggs, and the enzyme-rich vegetables greatly enhance digestion of protein.

Frittata with Asparagus and Fresh Dill ■ ■ ■ ■ ■ ■ ■

Ingredients:

4 tablespoons coconut oil or ghee

1 large onion, diced

3 large carrots, shredded

8 ounces zucchini, shredded

8 ounces yellow summer squash, shredded

1 large turnip, shredded

1 bunch asparagus, cooked and cut to
    ½-inch pieces

4 large eggs

1 teaspoon Celtic sea salt

¼ teaspoon cayenne pepper

2 tablespoons fresh dill

1 teaspoon paprika

Directions:

1. Preheat oven to 350 degrees.

2. Warm 2 tablespoons of coconut oil or ghee in a skillet and add onions. Sauté onions over medium-low heat until softened and translucent, about 7 minutes. Transfer to a bowl. Allow to cool and add carrots.

3. Place asparagus, zucchini, squash and turnip in a large strainer. Squeeze out excess water and add to the bowl of vegetables. Combine with eggs, salt, cayenne pepper, dill and paprika.

4. Brush a baking dish (or individual dishes or ramekins) with remaining coconut oil or ghee. Heat the dish in the oven for 5 minutes and then pour the egg mixture into the hot dish.

5. Set dish into a deeper baking dish and fill pan half way with very hot water. Bake 30 minutes or until top is browned and eggs are set.

Perfectly Poached Eggs ■ ■ ■ ■ ■ ■ ■

Ingredients:

3 or 4 large organic eggs

Directions:

1. Heat about 2 inches of water until bubbles cover the bottom and sides of pan.

2. Crack each egg into a separate small bowl, making sure yolks are intact.

3. Carefully pour each egg into the pan, leaving room between the eggs.

4. Cook eggs about 2 minutes, until whites set and yolks are still runny.

5. Remove eggs from water using a slotted spoon, or if necessary, use a wide rubber spatula.

If serving immediately, blot the bottom of the spoon on a paper towel to remove excess water before serving.

Softly Scrambled Eggs

Ingredients:

1 tablespoon raw butter or ghee

2 whole eggs plus 4 egg yolks

Splash of filtered water (to replace some of missing whites)

Herbamare™ or sea salt, to taste

Directions:

1. Combine eggs, water, sea salt or Herbamare in a bowl. Beat with a whisk or fork until well blended.

2. Melt butter or ghee in a nonstick frying pan over low to medium-low heat.

3. Add eggs, and using a flexible spatula carefully scrape eggs away from pan just as mixture begins setting on bottom and edges of pan.

4. When eggs are only two-thirds done, quickly remove the pan from the heat. The residual heat will continue to cook the eggs. After another minute of stirring, place eggs into the serving bowl and stir them around a few more times.

These scrambled eggs can be garnished with dulse flakes and/or chopped green onions. Serve with cultured vegetables. Eggs, especially when prepared this way with the extra egg yolks, nourish your thyroid and are truly "brain food."

Gluten-Free Pumpkin Flatcakes

Ingredients:

2 eggs

¼ cup pumpkin purée

⅛ teaspoon cinnamon

Coconut oil

Raw butter for serving

Directions:

1. Warm a cast iron pan over medium high heat.

2. Whisk together the eggs, pumpkin purée, and cinnamon.

3. Add coconut oil to the hot pan.

4. Use about 2 tablespoons of batter to make each flatcake.

5. Cook until golden on the bottom and the edges with a slightly opaque center.

6. Flip, brown the other side, and serve with butter.

Spinach Latkes

Ingredients:

2 cups spinach

½ large yellow onion, diced

6 ounces fresh shiitake mushrooms, de-stemmed and thinly sliced

4 tablespoons fresh chives

5 eggs

½ bunch parsley, roughly chopped

Celtic sea salt, to taste

2 tablespoons dried basil

1 teaspoon dill

1 teaspoon garlic powder

1 teaspoon dried oregano

3 tablespoons coconut oil or ghee

1 pinch cayenne pepper

Directions:

1. Blanch spinach in boiling water for 2 minutes. Drain in sieve and allow to cool, then press out excess water. Roughly chop and place in large mixing bowl.

2. Add chopped onion and sliced shiitake mushrooms to the chopped spinach.

3. Lightly beat eggs and add to spinach mixture. Add the dried and fresh herbs and salt. Mix well. Cover and chill in refrigerator 4 to 6 hours.

4. When ready, heat a large skillet over medium heat. Grease skillet with 2 teaspoons of coconut oil and pour ⅓ cup-sized portions into skillet.

5. If using an oven, preheat to 400 degrees. Using a small ladle, spoon batter onto a greased baking sheet. Bake for 10 minutes, or until browned and crisp.

These Body Ecology latkes are inspired by the traditional Jewish potato pancakes. These make a great brunch or lunch dish. Latkes are traditionally served with a sauce, but they can definitely stand alone.

Notes

Little Dishes ■ ■ ■ ■ ■ ■ ■

Little dishes can be eaten as snacks and, of course, make great appetizers. You can dress them up by simply calling them hors d'oeuvres.

Whatever you call them, little dishes are a must when entertaining. A delicious first course presented beautifully can be the perfect way to start a party and whet your guests' appetites for the main course. Or make them all ahead of time and serve them tapas-style for a ladies luncheon, bridal shower or fundraiser.

Have fun with these little dishes and while your health-conscious friends savor each bite they'll be delighted to know that you are not poisoning them with gluten, heavy cream, and mayonnaise made with trans-fatty acids.

Easy Veggie Chips   ■ ■ ■ ■ ■ ■ ■

Ingredients:

3 large zucchinis

3 large carrots

½ cup green onions, chopped

½ cup fresh dill

2 or 3 teaspoons celery seeds

1 tablespoon organic, unfiltered olive oil

Directions:

1. Shred the zucchinis and carrots in a food processor. Change blades if necessary, add remaining ingredients, and process for about 1 minute. The mixture should be slightly sticky.

2. Raw method: Spoon cracker-sized servings onto dehydrator sheets and dehydrate for 5 to 6 hours. Flip the chips every 2 hours.

3. Baked method: Spoon cracker-sized servings onto a greased pizza stone and bake on low for 2 to 3 hours, or until crispy. Flip the chips after 1 hour.

This nut-free, grain-free, seed-free snack is perfect for dipping into cultured veggies, on top of a salad, or just by the handful. Even the kids will love it.

The versatile zucchini squash makes a perfect addition to your healthy cracker and chip recipes. Have fun adding it to your favorite dehydrated and baked chip recipes for the extra benefit of dietary fiber.

Earth Day Crackers

Ingredients:

4 cups sprouted raw flax seeds

3 cups artichoke hearts

1 tablespoon turmeric

1 garlic clove

Celtic sea salt, to taste

4 cups cultured vegetables

Directions:

1. Process flax, artichoke hearts, turmeric, sea salt and garlic in a high-speed blender.

2. Stir in cultured vegetables and blend to desired texture.

3. Spoon onto dehydrator tray, shape into crackers, and dehydrate for 5 to 10 hours, depending on the texture you like.

Experiment with dill, cumin or other seasonings! Soaked nuts can be used instead of flax seeds, or try a mixture of flax and chia seeds.

Leek-Stuffed Squash Cups

Ingredients:

1 small winter squash, such as acorn or butternut, halved, seeded

1 cup filtered water

2 leeks (include some of the green part), cleaned, thinly sliced

2 ounces fresh shiitake mushrooms, de-stemmed, thinly sliced

1 tablespoon coconut oil or ghee

1 small zucchini, washed, cut into thin half moons

1 large garlic clove, minced

Directions:

1. Preheat oven to 350 degrees.

2. Place squash in an ovenproof baking dish, cut side down. Pour water into pan and bake for 60 to 75 minutes until meat is soft.

3. Remove squash from oven, drain water and set squash aside to cool.

4. Heat oil in small sauté pan over medium heat. Add leeks, garlic, and zucchini. Sauté for 5 to 7 minutes, or until fragrant and vegetables begin to soften.

5. Remove from heat and stir in mushrooms. Set aside for 15 minutes and allow residual heat to continue to cook the mixture.

6. Spoon stuffing into squash cups and return to baking dish, this time with cut side up. Bake at 400 degrees for 25 to 35 minutes.

Another great dish for entertaining! Make it the day of your party or a day in advance. Bake when you're ready! It is easy to double, triple or quadruple this recipe, so last-minute guests will not send you into a panic. The squash cups also make a very nice lunch served with spinach soup, or as a vegetarian entrée served with grains.

Red Bell Peppers Stuffed with Millet

■ ■ ■ ■ ■ ■ ■

Ingredients:

4 large red bell peppers, seeded, cut into quarters

1 teaspoon Celtic sea salt, or to taste

¼ teaspoon cayenne pepper

3 tablespoons coconut oil or ghee

1 medium yellow onion, finely chopped

2 ribs celery, finely chopped

3 cups millet, soaked for 8 hours and cooked

¼ cup fresh mint, coarsely chopped

2 tablespoons flat-leaf parsley, finely chopped

2 tablespoons capers, drained

3 tablespoons lemon juice, freshly squeezed

Directions:

1. Preheat oven to 400 degrees.

2. Sprinkle the peppers with ½ teaspoon Celtic sea salt.

3. Heat coconut oil in a large skillet over medium heat. Add the onion, celery, salt and cayenne pepper. Cover and cook, stirring occasionally, for about 4 minutes, or until the onion is softened.

4. Add cooked millet, mint, parsley, capers, lemon juice, and remaining salt. Stir to mix well and season to taste.

5. Stuff millet mixture into pepper quarters. Arrange peppers in a glass baking dish in one layer. Pour 1 cup of water around, not over, the peppers.

6. Cover pan tightly with foil and bake for about 1 hour, or until peppers are fork-tender.

Artichoke Paté Roll Up

■ ■ ■ ■ ■ ■ ■

Ingredients:

1 14-ounce can of artichokes, rinsed to remove citric acid

¼ cup water

¼ cup organic, unfiltered olive oil

¼ cup fresh organic lemon juice, or approximately the juice of 1 lemon

1 cup almonds, soaked for 8 hours

¼ red onion, coarsely chopped

2 tablespoons capers, soaked 8 hours to remove citric acid

½ teaspoon fine-grind Celtic sea salt

Pinch of garlic powder

Small, whole romaine leaves

Directions:

1. Purée all ingredients except lettuce leaves in a blender until creamy and smooth.

2. Place spoonful of mixture into lettuce leaf and roll up. Taste, and adjust sea salt if needed.

Chicken in Lettuce Leaf Wraps

■ ■ ■ ■ ■ ■ ■

Ingredients:

1½ pounds boneless, skinless chicken thighs or breasts

1 or 2 tablespoons coconut oil

¾ cup fresh shiitake mushrooms, de-stemmed, chopped

1 small red pepper, diced

½ cup daikon, chopped

½ cup green onions, sliced very thin

1 tablespoon ginger, minced

2 tablespoons coconut or brown rice vinegar

2 tablespoons wheat-free, low-sodium tamari

1 tablespoon Worcestershire sauce (Wizard's is wheat-free)

½ teaspoon garlic powder

¼ teaspoon crushed red pepper flakes

1½ cups carrots, shredded

½ cup green onions, julienned

12 Bibb or Boston lettuce leaves

⅓ cup sliced almonds, toasted (optional)

Directions:

1. Cook chicken in oven or sauté in coconut oil until only very slightly pink inside. Remove from heat and let stand until cool enough to handle. Cut into bite-size cubes.

2. Sauté mushrooms in 1 or 2 tablespoons of coconut oil for 3 minutes. Add cooked chicken, ginger, red pepper and scallions and sauté 4 to 6 minutes longer. (Make sure chicken is no longer pink.)

3. Drain and set aside.

4. Whisk together vinegar, tamari, Worcestershire sauce, garlic powder, red pepper flakes and remaining oil in a small bowl. Stir in carrots, onions, and chicken mixture. Fold in almonds, if using.

5. Spoon onto lettuce leaves and serve.

Harvest Grains Zucchini Boats

Ingredients:

4 large zucchinis

1 cup quinoa, soaked for 8 hours and cooked

¾ cup millet, soaked for 8 hours and cooked

¾ amaranth, soaked for 8 hours and cooked

¼ cucumber, diced

1 red onion, minced

2 tablespoons lemon juice, freshly squeezed

2 tablespoons cilantro, chopped

2 tablespoons mint, chopped

1 tablespoon coconut oil or ghee

2 teaspoons ground cumin

Celtic sea salt, to taste

Directions:

1. Preheat oven to 400 degrees.

2. Trim off top layer of each zucchini horizontally about ¼ inch. Gently scoop out the inner flesh and reserve.

3. Blanch and shock zucchini shells, set aside.

4. Combine reserved inner flesh of zucchini, quinoa, millet, amaranth, onion, lemon juice, herbs, coconut oil, and cumin in a bowl. Mix well and add salt to taste.

5. Fill zucchini shells with grain mixture so that they are slightly overflowing. Place them in a shallow baking pan.

6. Bake for 20 to 25 minutes, or until zucchini shells are tender and dish is hot all the way through.

Leek, Quinoa, and Mushroom Packets

Ingredients:

1 tablespoon coconut oil or ghee

2 cups leeks (include a little of the green part), cleaned, thinly sliced

2 cups fresh shiitake mushrooms, de-stemmed, thinly sliced

3 cups quinoa, soaked for 8 hours and cooked

1 onion, minced

1 large head savoy cabbage, large leaves separated, blanched until soft, chilled

3 tablespoons fresh dill

3 tablespoons fresh parsley

½ cup broth or homemade stock (page 57)

1½ cups Body Ecology's Gluten-Free Gravy (page 111)

Directions:

1. Sauté onions in coconut oil over medium heat until lightly golden. Add leeks and mushrooms. Continue to sauté for 5 minutes, or until tender.

2. Add quinoa and herbs. Remove from heat and set aside.

3. Place a scoop of filling into each cabbage leaf. Roll and set aside.

4. Bring broth to a simmer in a large skillet. Reduce heat to low and arrange cabbage rolls in skillet, seam side down. Cover and simmer 10 to 15 minutes, or until heated through.

5. Enjoy topped with Body Ecology's Gluten-Free Gravy.

Notes

Soups ■ ■ ■ ■ ■ ■ ■ ■ ■ ■ ■
High Protein Soups
Non-Starchy Vegetable Soups
Starchy Vegetable Soups

Mention the word soup and most people picture a steaming bowl of delicious, nutritious food, or they remember the great aromas that drew them to their mothers' kitchens, or they recall how a bowl of cold soup calmed them down on a hot summer day. Body Ecology has wonderful soups—they're simple to make, easy to digest, and very healing!

Traditionally, soup is served at lunch or dinner but we recommend that you eat it for breakfast, too. Soup has a high water content and is alkaline-forming, and it's ideal in the morning when your body is dehydrated. You can make your breakfast soup as light or as filling as you want; anything from a vegetable broth to a hearty soup with cut-up vegetables and even grains.

Soups are a godsend for busy people! Pull out that slow cooker you never use, and make soup in it while you're out working or running errands. You can make a large amount and keep it in the refrigerator for several days so that you always have a complete, healthy meal at your fingertips. When you have something like soup so available, it's easy to follow Body Ecology principles.

If you don't like to cook, or feel you're not particularly good at it, soups are foolproof. You can season them to your individual taste, add leftovers to fill them out, and change the flavors each time you make them. Be creative and daring—it's almost impossible to make a mistake! Children, who are often picky eaters, tend to love soup, especially if they help you make it.

Try a "clean out the refrigerator" soup. Look for vegetables or leftovers that need to be used soon and invent a soup with them. Or make a soup using scraps of onion skins, carrot peels, celery leaves, broccoli stems, cabbage cores, and fresh herbs. The skins and peels of vegetables contain extraordinary amounts of nutrients—but use them only if they are organic, because pesticides and toxins accumulate on the skins or in the areas between the root and leaves, like carrots.

Not sure how to use those good-for-you sea vegetables? Put several three-inch strips of kombu in the pot when you start your soup. When the soup is cooked, remove the strips, chop them, and return them to the pot.

If you have an especially weak intestinal tract, we highly recommend that you blend soups, which makes them even easier to digest. You can use a hand-held immersion blender to purée the soup right in the pot and save cleanup time.

Most of our soups taste terrific either hot or cold, so adjust them to the season. Our "cream" soups, such as Creamy Dilled Cauliflower (page 56), don't really use cream or any dairy ingredient; they are blended and only taste rich and creamy.

In vegetable soups (starchy or non-starchy), you can use a bit of butter, ghee, or preferably coconut oil. Warm the coconut oil, add onions and other vegetables and sauté for a few minutes, and then add your water or broth and seasonings. The sautéing, especially of the onions, yields a more flavorful soup. But if you are short on time, just put everything in the pot and cook.

Generally you should add salt during the final 10 to 20 minutes of cooking, or after puréeing, but if you want the vegetables to stay firm, add salt in the beginning. Add just enough to bring out flavor in the ingredients, but not enough for the soup to taste salty.

You can adapt many traditional soup recipes to Body Ecology Diet principles. So go to it, and have fun!

Using Garlic and Garlic Oil

For especially delicious soups—and as a real time saver—replace the garlic and oil in recipes with a combined garlic oil. We make garlic oil from whole heads of organic garlic and extra-virgin olive oil. It keeps well in a glass jar in the refrigerator, and you can use it to sauté onions and shallots for soups. Doing so seems to replace the "body" found in meat stocks without resorting to stocks that contain yeast or hydrolyzed vegetable protein, a naturally occurring MSG. This MSG is also found in all unfermented soy products, including Bragg Liquid Aminos.

To make garlic oil: Peel two entire heads (not just cloves) of garlic and place the cloves in a blender; pulse until coarsely chopped. Slowly add two cups of olive oil while blending. Pour into a glass jar and refrigerate until needed. If you own a hand-held blender, it's even easier. Simply chop the garlic in a wide-mouth glass jar, and then slowly add the oil while blending.

Garlic is excellent for warding off parasites, yeasts, and pathogenic bacteria. This great recipe idea isn't just for soups—use garlic oil to replace garlic and the oil or butter in any of our Body Ecology recipes.

Asparagus Soup

■ ■ ■ ■ ■ ■ ■

Ingredients:

3½ pounds fresh asparagus

3 large yellow onions, chopped

2 tablespoons coconut oil or ghee

5 cups homemade chicken stock or bone broth

Celtic sea salt and/or Herbamare to taste

Directions:

1. Cut off asparagus tips and set aside.

2. Cut spears into 1-inch pieces, discarding the tough ends.

3. Sauté onions in coconut oil or ghee until soft and golden.

4. Bring broth to a low simmer. Add cooked onions and asparagus spear pieces. Cook on low heat until asparagus is soft.

5. Purée, then return to heat and add asparagus tips. Add Herbamare and/or sea salt to taste.

6. Cook for 10 more minutes or just until tips are no longer crisp.

This soup is delicious hot or cold! Because of the chicken broth, it combines best with non-starchy vegetables.

Salmon with Kale Soup

■ ■ ■ ■ ■ ■ ■

Ingredients:

2 tablespoons coconut oil or ghee

1 large onion, cubed

3 carrots, chopped

1 large daikon radish, chopped

1 bunch kale, wash leaves but leave some water on leaves before chopping into small pieces

2 teaspoons dried dill

Spring water

2 7-ounce cans salmon (including bones)

3 or 4 lemon wedges

Celtic sea salt to taste

Directions:

1. Sauté onion in oil or ghee in a large saucepan.

2. Add carrots, daikon radish and kale and continue to sauté for several minutes. Add dill then cover saucepan and simmer on very low heat until kale is tender. (The water on the kale will help it steam as it cooks.)

3. Place cooked vegetables and salmon in a blender and process, adding spring water as necessary to create a creamy but thick soup. Blend until smooth. Return to saucepan.

4. Add sea salt to taste and simmer on very low heat until salmon is heated through, 5 to 10 more minutes.

5. Serve with lemon wedges.

Sea Bass Soup

■ ■ ■ ■ ■ ■ ■

Ingredients:

½ teaspoon Celtic sea salt

1 strip kombu

3 dried shiitake mushrooms

½ teaspoon coconut oil

½ pound fresh sea bass, cut into bite-size chunks

3 slices each of daikon and carrot, cut into bite-size chunks

Serve this soup hot for a great weekend brunch dish!

Directions:

1. Bring 3 inches of filtered water to a simmer in a shallow pan or stockpot. Add sea salt, kombu, shiitake mushrooms and coconut oil. Cover and let simmer for 30 to 40 minutes. The medicinal properties and the minerals of the kombu and the shiitake mushroom are now in the broth!

2. Add sea bass and chunks of daikon and carrot, if desired. Cover and continue to simmer approximately 10 minutes.

3. Remove from heat and let sit, covered, to finish cooking.

Seafood Donabe

■ ■ ■ ■ ■ ■ ■

Ingredients:

1 strip kombu, 2 or 3 inches long

6 dried shiitake mushrooms

1 tablespoon plus 1 teaspoon wheat-free tamari

2½ cups filtered water

1 teaspoon Herbamare

½ head cabbage, cut into 4 wedges

2 carrots, cut on diagonal into 2-inch pieces

1 small daikon, cut on diagonal into 2-inch pieces

½ block soft silken tofu, cut into ½-inch cubes

1 small head broccoli, cut into bite-size florets, stems removed

1 handful of baby spinach

2 pounds fresh sea bass, cut into 2-inch pieces

½ pound mussels (optional)

12 medium, shelled, raw shrimp

12 scallops

8 scallions, chopped

Directions:

1. Soak kombu and dried shiitake mushrooms in 2½ cups of water in a traditional Japanese donabe pot or a shallow 10-inch braiser or heavy pot for several hours or overnight.

2. Remove mushrooms, slice, and return to pot. Bring to a rapid simmer.

3. Add tamari, Herbamare, and wedges of cabbage. Simmer 3 minutes.

4. Reduce heat if necessary to maintain a gentle simmer and add remaining ingredients, arranging them attractively in the pot. Cover and cook for approximately 3 to 5 minutes or until mussels open and the other seafood is cooked.

5. Taste broth and adjust tamari and Herbamare if necessary.

Donabe meals usually feed four people and are served at the table, family-style. This version with fish and shellfish is an impressive entrée for a special occasion.

Fish Chowder

Ingredients:

1 tablespoon coconut oil or ghee

1 cup leeks or 1 whole onion, diced

1 garlic clove, minced

½ cup carrots, thinly sliced

½ cup celery, thinly sliced

2 cups homemade fish stock or vegetable stock

¼ cup parsley, chopped

8 tender celery leaves, chopped

1 ten-inch piece of daikon, diced

1 large bay leaf

2 whole cloves

¾ pound of white fish (see suggestions below), plus 1 small piece for stock

1/8 teaspoon kelp

1/8 teaspoon Celtic sea salt, or to taste

2 tablespoons parsley or chives, minced

Directions:

1. Sauté leek or onion and garlic in coconut oil or ghee over low heat. When slightly translucent, add carrots and celery and continue to sauté for several minutes.

2. Make fish stock (or use vegetable stock) with the small piece of fish and all remaining ingredients except parsley or chives. Simmer on low heat until vegetables are tender. Adjust seasonings if necessary. Remove and discard the small piece of fish, cloves, and bay leaf.

3. While stock is simmering, bake or sauté remaining fish, seasoning the fish to enhance flavor.

4. Remove 1 to 2 cups of soup and process in blender until creamy. Return to pan.

5. Cut baked or sautéed fish into bite-size pieces, add to broth, and cook gently for 5 to 6 minutes.

6. Garnish with minced parsley or chives and serve.

This soup is dairy-free, has no tomatoes, and is high in calcium! Any firm white fish such as sea bass, halibut, cod, grouper, snapper, rockfish, trout, turbot, perch, red rock or haddock will work for this recipe. You can also use salmon fillet. If the fish you choose has bones, pick them out carefully before using.

Remember that animal-protein soups should be combined with non-starchy vegetables, ocean vegetables, and/or raw salads.

Cooking Tip

Most fish soups call for cooking the fish for a long time as this helps flavor the stock. However, this makes the fish tough and difficult to digest. You want flavor in your broth, but you also want the fish to be tender. In this recipe use a smaller piece of fish in the stock and cook the rest of the fish in your oven or sauté it in a pan, seasoning it as desired. Then when you are ready to serve the fish soup, cut the fish into bite size pieces and add it to your hot soup broth. This method also allows you to season the fish nicely and adds extra flavor to the soup.

Broccoli and Fresh Fennel Soup   ■ ■ ■ ■ ■ ■ ■

Ingredients:

1 large head broccoli, separating florets and stems

1 large onion, chopped

4 to 6 garlic cloves, chopped

1 tablespoon coconut oil or ghee

Feathery tops from 1 bulb fresh fennel

6 cups filtered water

1 teaspoon ground fennel seed, or more to taste

Celtic sea salt or Herbamare to taste

Scallions and parsley, finely chopped

Red bell pepper, thinly sliced

Directions:

1. Peel broccoli stems and chop, discarding any woody pieces.

2. Sauté onion, garlic, and ground fennel seed in coconut oil or ghee in a stockpot. When onions are translucent, add broccoli stems and most of florets, reserving a handful of the smallest ones.

3. Add fennel tops and water and simmer until tender, about 20 minutes.

4. Purée mixture in blender or food processor for several minutes. Return to stockpot and add sea salt or Herbamare to taste.

5. Simmer 10 minutes and serve.

6. Garnish with reserved broccoli florets, parsley, scallions, and sliced red bell pepper strips.

This recipe is very popular as a breakfast soup. Fennel is an excellent digestive aid. Be sure to buy a bulb of fennel that has a generous amount of the feathery tops, which look a lot like fresh dill. Use the tops in this soup and save the bulb for later in another vegetable soup or a fresh salad.

Cauliflower Carrot Soup   ■ ■ ■ ■ ■ ■ ■

Ingredients:

1 tablespoon coconut oil or ghee

1 head of cauliflower, chopped

4 cups carrots, chopped

1 large onion, chopped

3 tablespoons fresh tarragon, chopped

Filtered water to cover

Celtic sea salt or Herbamare, to taste

Directions:

1. Heat coconut oil or ghee in a soup pot. Add onion and sauté until translucent.

2. Add carrots, cauliflower, fresh tarragon, and water. Simmer until tender, approximately 25 minutes.

3. Purée soup in blender and return to the pot. Add sea salt or Herbamare, as needed.

4. Simmer for 10 minutes and serve.

This is one of our most popular soups, and is great to serve to even your most difficult-to-please guests. It combines well with animal-protein or grain entrées. Make enough to have for several meals—it disappears quickly in our families!

Caramelized Onion Soup

Ingredients:

4 tablespoons coconut oil or ghee

1 pound Vidalia or other variety of sweet onions, thinly sliced

½ pound red onions, thinly sliced

½ cup shallots, thinly sliced

4 garlic cloves, minced

3 to 4 cups vegetable or chicken stock

1 tablespoon fresh thyme

Celtic sea salt, to taste

Directions:

1. Melt coconut oil or ghee over medium heat in a Dutch oven. Add onions and stir well to combine. Reduce heat to medium low. Cover and cook for 25 minutes or until very tender, stirring frequently.

2. Remove lid and increase heat to medium. Allow onions to slowly brown for 15 minutes, being careful to avoid burning them.

3. Add shallots and garlic and continue cooking for 2 minutes.

4. Add vegetable or chicken stock, thyme, and sea salt. Bring to a boil, reduce heat, cover and simmer for about 20 minutes, stirring occasionally.

Oil-Free Cauliflower and Carrot Soup

Ingredients:

8 cups filtered water

6 carrots, peeled and cut into thirds

2 heads cauliflower, cut into large florets

2 stalks celery, diced

1 large onion, cut into large chunks

4 garlic cloves, peeled

2 tablespoons Celtic sea salt

1 tablespoon dried parsley

1 teaspoon turmeric powder

1 teaspoon dried dill

Directions:

1. Bring water to a boil in a large stockpot. Add carrots and cover. After 5 minutes, add cauliflower and cook for 7 to 10 minutes. Next, add celery, onion, and whole garlic and cook for additional 5 to 7 minutes, or until celery is soft.

2. Turn off heat and add remaining ingredients.

3. Using either an immersion blender, a food processor, or a countertop blender, purée until creamy.

This tasty soup is non-dairy, uses no oil and is not overly sweet, as many carrot soups are. Add seasonings at the end of cooking because prolonged boiling can diminish flavor. We recommend allowing the soup to mellow overnight so that flavors have a chance to develop. If you can't wait until tomorrow, you can have a bowl today and serve the rest tomorrow!

If you are feeding a smaller group, this recipe is easily halved.

Creamy Dilled Cauliflower Soup

Ingredients:

1 tablespoon coconut oil or ghee

1 large onion, chopped

6 garlic cloves, minced

1 large head cauliflower, cut into chunks, reserving a handful of florets

6 tablespoons fresh dill

5 cups water

Celtic sea salt or Herbamare to taste

Directions:

1. Heat coconut oil or ghee in a stockpot. Add onion and sauté until translucent. Add garlic, cauliflower chunks, and fresh dill. Add just enough water to cover and simmer until ingredients are tender.

2. Purée with an immersion blender or in a countertop blender and return the soup to the stockpot. Add approximately 2 to 4 cups water, depending on desired consistency.

3. Season with sea salt or Herbamare, to taste. Add cauliflower florets and simmer until florets are tender.

A Medley of Greens Soup

Ingredients:

2 bunches kale, chopped

1 bunch collard greens, chopped

1 handful of baby spinach

1 large butternut squash, chopped

2 garlic cloves, minced

4 sprigs fresh rosemary

4 sprigs fresh thyme

2 teaspoons ground nutmeg

2 teaspoons Celtic sea salt

Coconut oil, to taste

Filtered water

Directions:

1. Place kale, collards, garlic and squash into a 4 quart pot. Cover with water and bring to a boil.

2. Reduce heat. Add spinach, herbs, nutmeg, and sea salt. Simmer for 5 to 10 minutes, and then remove from heat.

3. Add a few tablespoons of coconut oil. Use an immersion blender or a countertop blender to purée the soup. Enjoy with dollop of fermented vegetables.

Vegetarian Egg Drop Soup

■ ■ ■ ■ ■ ■ ■

Ingredients:

2 tablespoons coconut oil or ghee

12 garlic cloves, peeled and crushed

1 small onion, chopped

2 tablespoons arrowroot powder

1 tablespoon apple cider vinegar

4 cups vegetable stock

2 egg yolks

Directions:

1. Heat coconut oil or ghee in a stockpot. Add garlic cloves and onions, stir, cover, and cook over low heat for 20 minutes.

2. Dissolve arrowroot powder in vegetable stock and then stir in vinegar. Add to stockpot with garlic and onions. Simmer for 30 minutes.

3. Purée ingredients with immersion blender or countertop blender. Pour through a mesh sieve, and return to stockpot.

4. Just before serving, whisk in yolk. Avoid boiling.

Homemade Vegetable Stock

■ ■ ■ ■ ■ ■ ■

Ingredients:

2 tablespoons coconut oil

2 onions, chopped

1 turnip, chopped

4 celery stalks, chopped

2 carrots, chopped

1 strip of kombu

12 cups cold water

6 fresh parsley stalks

3 dried bay leaves

10 black peppercorns

Directions:

1. Heat the oil in a stockpot over medium-high heat. Add the onion, turnip celery, carrot, and kombu. Cook, stirring, for 5 minutes, or until browned.

2. Add the water, parsley, bay leaves and peppercorns and bring to a boil. Using a fine-slotted spoon or metal sieve, remove any scum that rises to the surface. Reduce heat to medium-low and simmer, uncovered, for 2 hours. Skim the surface every 30 minutes. Remove from heat and set aside for 30 minutes to cool slightly.

3. Place a fine sieve over a large heatproof bowl. Carefully strain stock through the sieve. Discard contents of sieve. Cool stock to room temperature.

4. Refrigerate or freeze in portions to suit your cooking needs. Freezing in ice cube trays may be handy for single-portion meals or when preparing food for an infant or young child.

If you don't have time to make your own stock, we recommend Marigold Organic Swiss Vegetable Bouillon (yeast-free and gluten-free), which comes in a package of eight cubes or powder. It is widely available in Australia and New Zealand or from amazon.com.

Vegetable and Kelp Noodle Soup

■ ■ ■ ■ ■ ■ ■

Ingredients:

6 dried shiitake mushrooms

4 cups homemade vegetable stock

1 16-ounce package of kelp noodles, soaked
    8 hours, rinsed, drained

1 scallion, sliced

¼ red bell pepper, diced

¼ teaspoon celery seed, ground

1 teaspoon garlic powder

2 tablespoons coconut oil or ghee

1 shredded carrot

Celtic sea salt, to taste

Directions:

1. Soak mushrooms at room temperature in vegetable stock until soft, or for about 30 minutes. When mushrooms are soft, drain and reserve vegetable stock. Slice mushrooms.

2. Combine scallion and red bell pepper in a bowl with shredded carrot, celery seed, and garlic powder. Set aside.

3. Heat oil or ghee in a stockpot over medium heat. Add vegetables and mushrooms and sauté for 3 to5 minutes, or just until vegetables begin to pop with color. Carefully add vegetable stock and bring to a boil.

4. Add kelp noodles and sea salt to taste, and simmer for 20 minutes.

You should add the sea salt while stock is simmering to chelate the salt's minerals into the rest of the ingredients. This delicious noodle soup combines well with animal protein. Go vegetarian or add chopped turkey sausage!

Gazpacho

■ ■ ■ ■ ■ ■ ■

Ingredients:

3 medium, ripe tomatoes

1 large cucumber

¼ of a small onion

1 clove garlic

1 stalk of celery

1 large Reed avocado, seeded and peeled

1 large lemon, juiced

Sea salt, to taste.

Filtered water

Directions:

1. Blend all ingredients in a blender. Add water to desired consistency. Serve chilled.

2. Season with the traditional flavors of parsley, sage, cilantro, and thyme.

Tomatoes are an acid fruit, not really a vegetable. We've included this recipe for tomato lovers, however, they're not for everyone. If tomatoes work for you, you'll enjoy this super easy, quick-to-fix, delicious summer soup.

Spinach and Coconut Soup

Ingredients:

2 bunches spinach, stems trimmed

1 tablespoon coconut oil or ghee

1 onion, chopped

2 garlic cloves, crushed

2 cups homemade vegetable stock

½ cauliflower, cut into florets

1 can of organic low-fat canned coconut milk, divided

¼ teaspoon ground nutmeg

½ teaspoon Celtic sea salt

1 pinch of cayenne pepper

Directions:

1. Rinse spinach leaves, and shake off excess water.

2. Melt coconut oil or ghee in a large saucepan over medium heat. Add onion and cook for 5 minutes or until tender. Add garlic and stir for 1 minute.

3. Add vegetable stock and cauliflower. Cover, bring to a boil, and cook for 8 minutes, or until cauliflower is tender. Add spinach and cook until just wilted.

4. Blend soup using a food processor, countertop blender, or immersion blender until smooth. Return to pan.

5. Add 1 cup of coconut milk, nutmeg, sea salt and cayenne pepper. Bring to a gentle simmer.

6. Ladle into cups and drizzle with remaining coconut milk. Season with a pinch of cayenne pepper.

Warming and delicious in cool weather, this spicy vegetable soup will leave you feeling "souper"!

Raw Garden Veggie Soup

Ingredients:

¾ cup coconut milk (page 27)

¾ cup filtered water

2 stalks celery

¼ yellow onion

1 cucumber, peeled

1 carrot, peeled

¼ red bell pepper, seeded

3 garlic cloves, peeled

2 tablespoons fresh lemon juice

¼ cup organic, unfiltered olive oil

1 teaspoon Celtic sea salt

½ bunch cilantro

Walnut or pumpkin seed oil

Directions:

1. Combine all ingredients, except walnut or pumpkin seed oil, in a high-speed blender and blend until smooth.

2. Pour into a serving bowl. Using a ladle, remove and discard any foam that rises to the top.

3. Garnish with a swirl of walnut or pumpkin seed oil.

Raw Cucumber Watercress Soup

■ ■ ■ ■ ■ ■ ■

Ingredients:

3½ cups cucumber juice, from 4 to 6
    cucumbers

⅓ cup freshly squeezed lemon juice

½ bunch fresh watercress

3 cloves garlic, peeled

2 tablespoons organic, unfiltered olive oil

2 teaspoons Celtic sea salt

Directions:

1. Using a juicer, juice the cucumbers.

2. In a high-speed blender, combine all of the ingredients and blend until smooth.

A light cucumber broth with fresh lemon and watercress is perfectly cooling for the summer.

Spinach Jade Soup

■ ■ ■ ■ ■ ■ ■

Ingredients:

4 tablespoons coconut oil or ghee

1 medium yellow onion, diced

5¼ cups homemade vegetable stock or
    Marigold Organic Swiss Vegetable Broth

Celtic sea salt, to taste

1 large carrot, diced

1 stalk of celery, diced

1 pound fresh spinach, washed, drained,
    stems removed

Directions:

1. Melt coconut oil or ghee in a large stockpot. Add onions and sauté until translucent.

2. Add stock, salt, carrot and celery. Cover and cook at a low simmer for approximately 20 minutes until carrots are tender.

3. Add spinach and cook until wilted.

4. Purée entire mixture in a blender. Serve hot.

Watercress Soup

■ ■ ■ ■ ■ ■ ■

Ingredients:

1 tablespoon coconut oil or ghee

1 large onion, chopped

5 garlic cloves, chopped

1 cup celery leaves

6 cups water

Celtic sea salt and Herbamare to taste

1 bunch watercress, washed, chopped, large
    stems removed

Directions:

1. Heat coconut oil or ghee in a stockpot. Sauté onion until translucent. Add garlic and celery tops and sauté gently for approximately 5 minutes more.

2. Add water, sea salt, and Herbamare and simmer for 10 minutes.

3. Purée soup with an immersion blender or a countertop blender until smooth. Return to stockpot and season according to taste.

4. Drop watercress into soup and bring to a boil. Remove from heat and cover with a lid until ready to serve.

A very elegant soup, and excellent to serve to dinner guests! This soup goes very well with animal-protein meals, and starchy vegetables and grains. Watercress is especially healing for the liver.

Basil Veggie Stew

■ ■ ■ ■ ■ ■ ■

Ingredients:

2 tablespoons coconut oil or ghee

1 large onion, chopped

3 tablespoons dried basil

3 large carrots, diced

3 potatoes, diced the same size as carrots

2 cups of water

2 teaspoons Celtic sea salt, or Herbamare to taste

1 small head cauliflower, chopped into florets

Directions:

1. Sauté onion and basil in coconut oil or ghee in a deep skillet until onions are translucent. Add carrots and potatoes and continue to sauté on low heat for 5 minutes. Add water, sea salt or Herbamare and cover. Cook on low heat for 20 minutes, or until vegetables are almost tender.

2. Drop cauliflower into pot and adjust seasonings, if necessary. Cover and cook until cauliflower is tender.

Butternut Squash Soup

■ ■ ■ ■ ■ ■ ■

Ingredients:

2 tablespoons coconut oil or ghee

1 large onion, halved and sliced

1 Marigold Organic Swiss Bouillon cube (optional)

7 cups filtered water

1 leek, chopped

2 cloves garlic

1 butternut squash, peeled, cubed

1/8 teaspoon allspice

1/8 teaspoon nutmeg

1/8 teaspoon ginger

Cayenne pepper, pinch

1/2 teaspoon Celtic sea salt

Herbamare to taste

3 tablespoons fresh dill, chopped as a garnish

Directions:

1. Heat coconut oil or ghee in a stockpot. Sauté onions until translucent. Add vegetable bouillon cube (if using) and water. Simmer for 10 minutes on medium-low heat.

2. Add leek, garlic, squash, spices, and sea salt. Continue to cook until squash is tender.

3. Purée using a blender or an immersion blender and adjust seasonings. Add Herbamare to taste.

4. Serve hot or cold, garnished with freshly chopped dill.

Curried Celery Soup ■ ■ ■ ■ ■ ■ ■

Ingredients:

2 tablespoons coconut oil or ghee

1 onion, chopped

1 leek, washed, sliced (reserve two dark green leaves)

1½ pounds celery, chopped

1 tablespoon curry powder

3 red-skin potatoes

3¾ cups homemade vegetable stock or filtered water

1 *bouquet garni*

2 tablespoons mixed fresh herbs, finely chopped

Celtic sea salt and Herbamare, to taste

Celery leaves, finely chopped

Pinch of celery seeds

An unusual blend of flavors, this soup is an excellent winter warm-up. Celery is rich in sodium and supports adrenal health.

Directions:

1. Heat the coconut oil or ghee in a large saucepan. Add the onion, leek and celery. Cover and cook gently for about 10 minutes, stirring occasionally. Add the curry powder and cook for an additional 2 minutes.

2. Make *bouquet garni*: Place a bay leaf, a sprig of thyme, and a sprig of parsley on reserved green leek leaf. Cover with remaining piece of green leek. Tie securely with fine string, leaving a length of string attached for easy retrieval.

3. Add potatoes, vegetable stock, and *bouquet garni*. Cover and bring to a boil. Simmer for 20 minutes, until the vegetables are tender.

4. Remove and discard the *bouquet garni*. Purée soup using an immersion blender or a countertop blender.

5. Return puréed soup to the saucepan and add the mixed herbs. Correct seasonings if necessary and reheat gently.

6. Ladle into soup bowls and garnish each with a sprinkling of celery seeds and the celery leaves.

Harvest Soup ■ ■ ■ ■ ■ ■ ■

Ingredients:

2 tablespoons coconut oil or ghee

1 large onion, chopped

3 garlic cloves, minced

5 medium carrots, chopped

3 red-skin potatoes, chopped

1 fennel bulb with stalk and leaves, chopped

1 bunch of broccoli, stems chopped, florets reserved for another use

Filtered water

Curry powder, to taste

Celtic sea salt and Herbamare, to taste

Directions:

1. Heat coconut oil or ghee in a stockpot. Sauté onion until translucent. Add other vegetables, curry powder, sea salt, Herbamare, and enough water to cover. When vegetables are tender, purée ingredients using an immersion blender or a countertop blender. Return soup to the stockpot.

2. If necessary, add more water to achieve desired consistency. Adjust seasonings, if necessary.

3. Simmer for 10 minutes and serve.

English Pea Soup

Ingredients:

2 tablespoons coconut oil or ghee

1 onion, diced

1 bay leaf

3 leeks, diced, white part only

1 cup celery, diced

1 small head of lettuce, such as romaine, Boston, butter or oak leaf

2 sprigs parsley

4 cups filtered water

3 cups frozen or fresh peas

1 teaspoon Celtic sea salt

Herbamare, to taste

Directions:

1. Sauté onion and bay leaf in coconut oil or ghee until onion is translucent. Add leeks, celery, lettuce and parsley. Sauté until tender.

2. Add 2½ cups water and 2 cups peas. Cover and simmer until peas are very soft. Purée soup in a countertop blender or with an immersion blender.

3. Meanwhile, simmer 1 cup of peas in 1½ cups water with ½ teaspoon sea salt, until peas are tender. Add to puréed soup.

4. Season with sea salt and Herbamare to taste. Simmer for 10 minutes and serve.

Cooked peas become starchy, so eat this as an entrée with non-starchy vegetables. This soup is also delicious served chilled in the summer.

Potato Corn Chowder

Ingredients:

2 tablespoons coconut oil or ghee

1 onion, diced

1 teaspoon thyme

2 bay leaves

6 cloves garlic

4 medium red-skin potatoes, diced

4 cups corn, divided

6 cups filtered water

1 tablespoon Celtic sea salt

1 leek, washed, halved lengthwise, sliced

3 stalks celery, diced

Directions:

1. Sauté onion with thyme, bay leaves, and garlic in coconut oil or ghee until onion is translucent.

2. Add potatoes, 2 cups corn, water, and sea salt. Simmer until potatoes are tender, approximately 20 minutes. Remove and discard bay leaves.

3. Purée 1½ cups of soup in a blender and return to pot. Add remaining corn, leeks, and celery. Simmer until veggies are tender, about 10 to 15 minutes.

Lima Bean Cilantro Soup

■ ■ ■ ■ ■ ■ ■

Ingredients:

2 tablespoons coconut oil or ghee

2 large onions, minced

8 cloves garlic, minced

4 carrots, halved

2 ten-ounce packages frozen lima beans

8 cups filtered water

2 teaspoons Celtic sea salt, or to taste

Pinch red pepper flakes (optional)

1 bunch cilantro, coarsely chopped

Directions:

1. Heat coconut oil or ghee in a stockpot. Sauté onions and garlic until translucent. Add carrots, lima beans, water, and sea salt. Simmer until vegetables are tender. Remove carrots, cool, and slice into thin rounds.

2. Purée approximately ¾ of soup in a blender and return to pot with carrots. Add red pepper flakes and additional sea salt, as desired.

3. Garnish with cilantro.

Potato Leek Soup

■ ■ ■ ■ ■ ■ ■

Ingredients:

1 leek, washed, halved lengthwise, sliced

1 pound red-skin potatoes, diced

2 carrots, diced

1 small piece celery root (celeriac), peeled and diced

Celtic sea salt, to taste

1 tablespoon fresh parsley, chopped

Directions:

1. Place all vegetables in a saucepan with enough cold, filtered water to cover. Bring to a boil, cover, and simmer over medium heat until soft.

2. Season with sea salt, according to taste. Sprinkle with chopped parsley before serving.

Gingery Acorn Squash Soup

■ ■ ■ ■ ■ ■ ■

Ingredients:

2 tablespoons coconut oil or ghee

1 acorn squash, peeled, seeded, chopped

2 medium carrots, chopped

2 medium onions, chopped

2 celery sticks, chopped

3 garlic cloves, minced

Thumb-size piece of ginger, peeled, grated

Filtered water

Celtic sea salt or Herbamare, to taste

Parsley, minced

Directions:

1. Heat coconut oil or ghee in a saucepan. Sauté onions until translucent then add celery, garlic, squash, ginger, and filtered water to cover. Simmer for 30 minutes or pressure-cook for 12 minutes.

2. Purée in a blender. Add water, if desired. Return to pan and season with sea salt or Herbamare, to taste. Simmer for 10 minutes.

3. Serve garnished with parsley.

Summer Corn Stew

■ ■ ■ ■ ■ ■ ■

Ingredients:

3 tablespoons coconut oil or ghee

1 large onion, diced

3 celery stalks, diced

2 cups of cilantro, chopped, divided

5 ears yellow corn, kernels removed, reserve cobs

5 potatoes, diced

1 red pepper, diced

8 cups of filtered water

2 teaspoons Celtic Sea Salt, or to taste

Herbamare, to taste

Directions:

1. Melt coconut oil or ghee over medium heat in a large stockpot. Sauté onions, celery, and half of cilantro until soft. Add potatoes, corncobs, sea salt, and water. Simmer until potatoes are soft.

2. Remove corncobs then add corn, red pepper, and remaining cilantro. Adjust seasonings, adding more sea salt and Herbamare to taste, if desired.

3. Remove soup from heat, and let sit covered for 10 minutes before serving.

Authentic Peruvian Quinoa Soup

■ ■ ■ ■ ■ ■ ■

Ingredients:

2 tablespoons coconut oil or ghee

2 large onions, chopped

2 large leeks, chopped

2 stalks celery, chopped

3 carrots, cut into 1½-inch matchsticks

5 garlic cloves, minced

1 large red bell pepper, seeded, chopped

1 cup peas, shelled

2 red-skin potatoes, diced

½ medium butternut squash, peeled, seeded, diced

½ head small cabbage, coarsely chopped

1 large bunch cilantro, stemmed, leaves chopped

1 cup fresh parsley, chopped

1 teaspoon cumin

1 cup quinoa, soaked 8 hours

8 cups water

Celtic sea salt or Herbamare, to taste

Directions:

1. Sauté the garlic, onions, leeks, and celery in coconut oil or ghee for several minutes. Add other ingredients and simmer until tender.

2. Add sea salt or Herbamare during last 10 minutes of cooking.

Extremely healing and easy to digest, this soup is a hearty meal. Accompany it with a raw leafy green salad or some cultured vegetables for even better nutritional balance.

Notes

Notes

Salads

What would we do without our salads? Salads can be a meal in themselves. They can be made with raw or cooked and chilled ingredients. They are simple to prepare, adhere easily to food-combining rules, and can be a staple in a health-building diet.

Raw foods, including raw salads, are difficult to digest when you have a compromised digestive tract. If this describes you then skip over many of the recipes in this section for now. However salads are such a great way to obtain a variety of colorful vegetables in your diet and they are so rich in enzymes, vitamins, and minerals that you'll want to add them to your diet as soon as you are able.

In spite of what many believe, salads do not have to have lettuce! Actually, lettuce is hard to digest so if you are using it in a salad take the time to chop it into smaller pieces (as in the famous "chopped salad" recipes). For easier digestion, make no-lettuce salads with a combination of finely chopped raw veggies (carrots, cucumbers, celery, jicama) tossed with coarsely chopped parboiled vegetables (broccoli, cauliflower, asparagus, green beans). Add your favorite salad dressing, of course. Oil-sensitive folks will find delicious no-oil dressings throughout this section.

On hot summer days crisp, cool salads are ideal. And year-round, you can easily carry them to work, with the dressing separate to add at the last moment. At Body Ecology, we are constantly striving to create balance in every meal and foods can either be expansive or contracting. If your body becomes contracted from eating too much salt or from a stressful day, balance the feeling of being tense with an expansive salad. And if your body is too acidic, an alkaline salad can be the perfect solution to come to the rescue.

Have your own salads gotten boring? We hope that after perusing our Body Ecology friendly recipes that the great variety of available lettuces and land, ocean, and cultured vegetables will inspire you. The more color, the better: fresh green broccoli, asparagus, and English peas; yellow summer squash and onions; bright red bell peppers or radishes; cool white cucumber or jicama! You can make grain salads with the four Body Ecology grains, as well as red-skin potatoes, or protein salads with chopped salmon, tuna, chicken or turkey. Or mix some soaked almonds, or sunflower or pumpkin seeds in with those veggie salads for extra crunch.

Tossing a spoonful or two of cultured vegetables into your salad provides an unexpected but delicious burst of flavor. Raw cultured vegetables add color and zest to any salad. We even add them to our mayonnaise and dressing recipes!

Please don't forget those very special ocean vegetables. The recipe "Hijiki with Onions and Carrots" (page 129) is delicious tossed into a leafy green lettuce and radicchio salad, then topped with The Body Ecology Diet Salad Dressing (page 94). Or soak some arame in water for ten minutes, then drain, chop, and add it to a chopped salad. Wakame is delicious in a cucumber salad with diced red bell pepper and red onion. Crumble sheets of nori into small pieces and sprinkle on any salad for a bit more color and a salty taste.

Build Your Favorite Body Ecology Salad ▪ ▪ ▪ ▪ ▪ ▪

Create a variety of your favorite salads by combining any or all of the following vegetables and herbs for an endless number of possibilities. Creating your own salad is easy and customized ingredients will provide a variety of alkaline-forming deliciousness!

START WITH THE BASICS
Lettuce varieties (romaine, Boston, Bibb)   Mixed field greens

OPTIONAL GREENS
(Use sparingly. These greens are either high in oxalates or are cruciferous vegetables and can suppress the thyroid.)

Arugula	Dandelion greens	Spinach	Watercress
Beet tops	Radish tops	Turnip tops	

SPROUTS

Alfalfa	Broccoli	Radish	Sunflower

STEMS AND ROOTS

Broccoli, steamed only	Celery	Jicama, shredded
Carrots, shredded	Corn, blanched	Summer squash
Cauliflower, steamed only	Jerusalem artichokes, shredded	Zucchini

ESPECIALLY NUTRITIOUS ADDITIONS

Arame, soaked or cooked	Nori, shredded	Scallions
Chives	Red onions	Wakame, soaked
Hijiki, cooked		

SEED AND HERB SEASONING CHOICES FOR SALAD DRESSINGS

Basil	Cinnamon	Onion powder	Sage
Cardamom	Garlic powder	Paprika	Thyme
Caraway	Horseradish	Parsley	Dill Turmeric
Cayenne	Marjoram	Poppy seeds	
Celery	Nutmeg	Pumpkin seeds	

HIGH QUALITY PROTEIN

Chicken	Fish (fresh or canned)	Bison	Chicken or turkey sausage
Eggs	Steak	Sliced lamb	

Asparagus, Green Bean, and Artichoke Salad ■ ■ ■ ■ ■ ■

Salad:

1 pound fresh, cooked asparagus spears, chilled slightly

½ pound fresh green beans, cooked, chilled slightly

½ head cauliflower, broken into small florets, steamed until fork tender, shocked in cold water, chilled slightly

6 small canned artichokes, drained, rinsed or frozen artichoke hearts, defrosted

½ cucumber, peeled, thinly sliced

1 red bell pepper, julienned

Dressing:

½ cup organic, unfiltered olive oil or flax oil

¼ cup raw, organic apple cider vinegar

½ teaspoon Celtic sea salt, or to taste

1 tablespoon dried basil, or to taste

Directions:

1. Combine olive oil, apple cider vinegar, sea salt, and basil in a screw-top jar. Shake well, and then chill.

2. Toss asparagus, green beans and cauliflower together in a salad bowl.

3. Add chilled dressing and toss gently.

4. Line a platter with thinly sliced cucumbers and arrange tossed salad ingredients in the center. Top with artichokes.

This elegant salad can stand alone or as a part of an alkaline-forming, all-vegetable meal. It is also delightful with a grain or grain-like seed entrée. Artichokes are a starchy vegetable, so remember not to serve this salad with animal protein. Instead, serve with quinoa, buckwheat or millet, or in Stage 2, with a grain.

Marinated Corn Salad ■ ■ ■ ■ ■ ■

Salad:

1 ¾ cups yellow corn, freshly cut from cob (about 4 ears)

¼ cup filtered water

½ small red bell pepper, cut into ½-inch strips

½ cup celery, chopped

2 tablespoons scallions, thinly sliced

1 tablespoon pimiento, chopped

1 tablespoon fresh parsley, chopped

Marinade:

3 tablespoons organic, unrefined flax or pumpkin seed oil

1 tablespoon raw, organic apple cider vinegar

Celtic sea salt, to taste

Directions:

1. Combine corn and water in a medium saucepan. Bring to a boil. Cover, reduce heat, and simmer 7 to 8 minutes or until corn is tender. Drain corn and combine with bell pepper and next 4 ingredients and set aside.

2. Combine oil, vinegar and sea salt in a jar; cover tightly and shake vigorously.

3. Add marinade to corn mixture. Cover and chill at least 4 hours before serving.

The Great Side Salad

■ □ ■ ■ ■ □ ■

Salad:

2 quarts filtered water

1 carrot, cut on the bias

1 head broccoli, cut into florets

1 head cauliflower, cut into florets

½ red onion, diced

2 scallions, thinly sliced

½ daikon radish, cubed

1 large head romaine lettuce, torn into bite-size pieces

2 cups baby arugula

2 cups spring mix lettuce

½ cup red bell pepper, cut into strips

Directions:

1. Bring 2 quarts filtered water to a boil in a stockpot. When water is boiling, blanch the carrots, broccoli, and cauliflower, one type of vegetable at a time, for about 2 to 3 minutes each until the colors become vibrant. Shock in cold water and drain well.

2. Combine all raw and blanched ingredients in a large bowl and toss with your favorite dressing.

Coleslaw Made Right!

■ □ ■ ■ ■ ■ ■

Salad:

1 small head green cabbage

2 cups filtered water

3 carrots, grated

Celtic sea salt to taste

6 cups water

2 teaspoons Celtic sea salt

Dressing:

Classic Homemade Mayonnaise (page 94), Almond Mayonnaise (page 95), or The Body Ecology Diet Salad Dressing (page 94)

Directions:

1. Cut cabbage in chunks and grate in a food processor or by hand.

2. Place cabbage in a large mixing bowl.

3. Bring water to boil in a large pot and add sea salt.

4. Choose a method to parboil cabbage:

   • Pour boiling salted water over cabbage chunks and let sit for 10 minutes; or

   • Cover cabbage chunks with water and salt and bring to a boil. Remove from heat, let stand 4 to 5 minutes.

5. Drain cabbage and chill.

6. Toss cabbage and carrots with dressing of your choice. Mix well. Chill until ready to serve.

Other raw ingredients can be added to the slaw, such as scallions, red bell peppers, celery, sliced daikon or red radishes, dill, caraway or celery seeds, sunflower seeds, chopped parsley, chives, fennel, or other fresh herbs.

For a sweeter coleslaw, add several drops of Body Ecology's stevia liquid concentrate to the mayonnaise before tossing with the veggies.

Zesty Zucchini Insalata ■ ■ ■ ■ ■ ■

Salad:

1½ pounds zucchini, grated

1 medium Vidalia or other sweet onion,
    thinly sliced

1½ teaspoons Celtic sea salt

1 red bell pepper, julienned

¼ cup raw, organic apple cider vinegar

3 tablespoons lemon juice (a Meyer lemon is
    delicious!)

2 tablespoons fresh basil, chopped

2 tablespoons mint, chopped

Celtic sea salt, to taste

Grated lemon zest from one small lemon

Directions:

1. Toss zucchini and onion with salt in a colander. Let mixture drain for 30 minutes. Rinse and squeeze to remove excess liquid. Transfer to a large bowl.

2. Add bell pepper, apple cider vinegar, lemon juice, basil and mint. Toss well. Season to taste and serve immediately, garnished with lemon zest.

Cool As A Cucumber Salad ■ ■ ■ ■ ■ ■

Salad:

3 large cucumbers, peeled, seeded

1 large carrot

½ red bell pepper, minced

½ white onion

Dressing:

3 to 4 tablespoons raw, organic apple cider
    vinegar

Celtic sea salt, to taste

Directions:

1. Cut cucumbers lengthwise and then into thin half-moons.

2. Cut onion into fine strips.

3. Use a peeler to make fine strips of the carrot.

4. Toss cucumbers, carrots, bell pepper and onions in a bowl. Sprinkle with sea salt and set aside for 10 minutes.

5. Sprinkle with vinegar and chill for 2 to 4 hours. Toss and serve.

Grated Carrots with Olive and Coconut Oils ■ ■ ■ ■ ■ ■

Salad:

4 to 6 large carrots, peeled, finely grated

2 tablespoons coconut oil

1 tablespoon organic, unfiltered olive oil

Dressing:

1 lemon, juiced

Herbamare to taste

Directions:

1. Combine carrots, lemon juice and both oils and toss.

2. Sprinkle with lemon juice and Herbamare

Green Bean Salad with Corn and Basil

Salad:

2 pounds green beans, trimmed

3 ears fresh corn, kernels removed, or use 10 ounces frozen corn

½ large red bell pepper, chopped

½ small red onion, chopped

⅓ cup basil, chopped

Hot sauce

Celtic sea salt

Dressing:

¼ cup organic, unfiltered olive oil

3 tablespoons raw, organic apple cider vinegar

3 tablespoons lemon juice

Directions:

1. Separately blanch green beans and corn kernels. Drain.

2. Toss all ingredients in a large bowl.

3. Season with hot sauce and sea salt.

Parboiled Salad

Salad:

Variety of lettuces, torn into bite-size pieces

Vegetables of your choice, parboiled, chopped:

Broccoli	Peas
Cabbage	Radishes
Carrots	Red onions
Celery	Scallions
Corn kernels	String beans
Cucumbers	Yellow squash
Daikon	Zucchini
Kale	

Vegetables are best when taken out of the water right after they have turned their brightest color (e.g., when broccoli turns a beautiful bright green, and is tender but still crunchy).

Directions:

1. Cut vegetables of your choice into pretty shapes (matchsticks, half-moons, flowers, stars). Use a vegetable cutter if you wish.

2. Parboil veggies in rapidly boiling salted water. When just tender, drain, immediately rinse in cold water, and then chill.

3. Put lettuce and chilled vegetables in a bowl. Toss with salad dressing of your choice and serve.

Did You Know?

Cruciferous vegetables like cabbage, kale, broccoli, and cauliflower should be parboiled until tender and then chilled before using in a salad. Raw cruciferous vegetables suppress the thyroid. On The Body Ecology Diet, we love cruciferous vegetables, but we ferment or cook them.

Summer Spaghetti Salad

■ ■ ■ ■ ■ ■

Salad:

2 seven-ounce packages Angel Hair Miracle Noodles or konjaku noodles

2 teaspoons sea salt or 1 tablespoon of wheat-free tamari

Coconut oil, for cooking

4 garlic cloves, chopped

1½ teaspoons dried rosemary

1½ teaspoons dried thyme

2 large handfuls of kale, chopped

1 small red bell pepper, diced

1 small zucchini, diced

1 small yellow summer squash, diced

3 to 4 tablespoons fresh basil, minced

Dressing:

5 tablespoons organic, unfiltered olive oil

4 tablespoons lemon juice, or more to taste

1 teaspoon Celtic sea salt, or to taste

Herbamare to taste

Dulse flakes

Directions:

1. Bring water to a simmer and add noodles, sea salt or tamari. Gently simmer for 10 minutes. Drain, cool, and cut the noodles with kitchen shears, if desired.

2. Heat coconut oil over low heat. Lightly sauté the garlic, rosemary, and thyme. Gradually add kale and stir until very soft. Remove from heat and cool.

3. Pour olive oil and lemon juice over noodles and using your hands gently mix in red bell peppers, zucchini, yellow squash, sea salt and basil. Add kale and herbs.

4. Taste and adjust seasonings, adding Herbamare to taste. Serve with a sprinkling of dulse flakes.

Summer Spaghetti Salad is delicious when served with your favorite probiotic beverage or fermented, cultured vegetables. It's a simple, scrumptious, gluten-free recipe if you're looking for a healthy alternative to spaghetti noodles made with wheat. We recommend Miracle Noodle (www.miraclenoodle.com).

Totally free of carbohydrates, Miracle Noodles are made of shirataki, a favorite Japanese food because it provides fiber for healthy digestion. This fiber is also called glucomannan or konjaku, and can now be easily purchased here in the U.S. at grocery stores or www.miraclenoodle.com . It is used in weight loss programs, and research shows it plays a role in regulation of blood sugar and cholesterol. In Stage 2 of The Body Ecology Diet, this salad can be made with rice noodles.

Carrot Salad with Cumin

■ ■ ■ ■ ■ ■

Salad:

1 pound carrots, coarsely grated

½ cup fresh parsley, chopped

1 tablespoon lemon juice

2 tablespoon organic, unfiltered olive oil

1 garlic clove, minced

½ teaspoon cumin

Celtic sea salt, to taste

Directions:

1. Combine all ingredients in a bowl.

2. Allow flavors to blend for 3 hours in refrigerator before serving.

Jicama Salad

Salad:

1 cup red onion, chopped

2 limes, juiced

1 teaspoon Celtic sea salt

2 cups jicama, chopped

1 red bell pepper, chopped

1 bunch cilantro, chopped

1 avocado, cubed

½ teaspoon turmeric

½ teaspoon cumin

½ teaspoon cayenne pepper

Directions:

1. Place onion, lime juice and sea salt in a mixing bowl and mash with a fork. Add jicama, bell pepper, cilantro and avocado. Sprinkle with turmeric, cayenne pepper, and cumin and stir well. Add more lime if needed.

2. Muddle the ingredients with a fork, so that the flavors penetrate the jicama.

Serve this flavorful salad with homemade Earth Day Crackers (page 42) or blend with some cultured vegetables!

Spring Dragon Kelp Noodle Salad

Salad:

6 ounces kelp noodles

2 scallions, thinly sliced

1 large red bell pepper, sliced

½ bunch cilantro, roughly chopped

½ bunch parsley, roughly chopped

½ bunch chives, minced

1 garlic clove, finely minced

Dressing:

3 tablespoons MCT Oil

4 tablespoons organic, unfiltered olive oil

Celtic sea salt, to taste

Cayenne pepper, to taste

This extremely healthy salad is served cold, and keeps well.

Directions:

1. Rinse kelp noodles in fresh water. Cut the noodles with kitchen shears, if desired. Transfer to a large serving bowl.

2. Add scallions, bell pepper, cilantro, parsley, chives and garlic to the noodles.

3. Drizzle salad with the oils, sea salt and cayenne pepper. Toss well to coat.

4. Refrigerate for at least 1 hour before serving to allow flavors to blend.

Kelp noodles are a sea vegetable in the form of a noodle. Their neutral taste allows for a variety of uses. including salads, soups, stir-fries, and casseroles. They are a tasty, nutritious alternative to pasta and rice noodles, and a rich source of iodine. (More information is available at www.kelpnoodles.com).

The MCT Oil is a super healthy oil derived from coconut and palm oil. The one we use is Brain Octane Oil from Upgraded™ Bulletproof® available at www.upgradedself.com.

Summertime Curried Corn Salad

■ ▨ ■ ■ ■ ■

Salad:

6 to 8 ears corn, kernels removed, or 3 cups frozen corn

1 small zucchini, diced

1 large red bell pepper, diced

1 bunch scallions, white and tender part of green, cut into ¼ inch pieces

½ cup Italian parsley, chopped

Dressing:

¼ cup organic, unrefined flax or pumpkin seed oil

4 tablespoons raw, organic apple cider vinegar or lemon juice

1 teaspoon curry powder

½ teaspoon Celtic sea salt

1 to 2 garlic cloves, minced

Directions:

1. Use the corn raw or blanch it quickly and cool. Combine the corn, zucchini, pepper, scallions, and parsley in a bowl.

2. Whisk the oil, vinegar or lemon juice, curry powder, sea salt and garlic in a small bowl. Add to the vegetables and toss gently. Marinate for 2 to 4 hours before serving.

Add 1 to 2 tablespoons of Classic Homemade Mayonnaise (page 94) for a creamier dressing.

Sweet Carrot "Gelatin" Salad

■ ▨ ■ ■ ■ ■

Salad:

3½ cups filtered water

1 tablespoon agar powder, or 4 tablespoons agar flakes

Zest of 1 lemon

¼ teaspoon Celtic sea salt

2 stalks celery, finely shredded

3 medium carrots, shredded

3 to 6 drops stevia liquid concentrate, or to taste

½ cup lemon and/or lime juice

Directions:

1. Dissolve agar in 2 cups cold filtered water in a saucepan. Add lemon zest and sea salt. Bring to a boil, then boil for 5 minutes. Add celery and boil 1 minute more. Add carrots, stevia, 1½ cups filtered water, and continue boiling 3 minutes more until carrots are desired consistency. Mix well. Add lemon juice.

2. Pour mixture into mold, bowl, or square baking dish. Allow to set.

3. Unmold and serve on bed of lettuce with a dollop of Classic Homemade Mayonnaise (page 94).

Looking for something to bring to your summer get-togethers? This recipe is great for potlucks. If you increase the amount of ingredients, do not increase the amount of stevia. Always be sure to test for taste.

Red Potato Salad in Red Onion Dressing

■ ■ ■ ■ ■ ■

Salad:

2 pounds small red-skin potatoes

Celtic sea salt or Herbamare, to taste

Dressing:

½ cup red onion, finely chopped

½ cup dill, fennel, or parsley, minced

¾ cup Classic Homemade Mayonnaise (page 94)

Fresh dill or parsley sprigs for garnish

Directions:

1. Cut potatoes into bite-size cubes and cook until tender.

2. Cool potatoes and add all other ingredients.

3. Chill before serving. Garnish with fresh herbs.

Add watercress, mustard, and 1 or 2 tablespoons of raw, organic apple cider vinegar, or herbs such as curry powder, garlic, Italian seasonings, etc. Toss in several spoonsful of your favorite cultured veggie blend to give this salad even more pizzazz—and, of course, make it more digestible, too.

These same ingredients can be tossed with The Body Ecology Diet Salad Dressing (page 94) instead of the mayonnaise, and it's even healthier.

Avocado and Grapefruit Salad

■ ■ ■ ■ ■ ■

Salad:

2 red grapefruits

2 Hass avocados, peeled, pitted and sliced

¼ small red onion, finely diced

Several leaves of Bibb or Butter lettuce per person

Coarsely chopped arugula to garnish

Dressing:

Dollop of mayonnaise for each plate. Make Classic Homemade Mayonnaise (page 94) or use Follow Your Heart ™ Grapeseed Oil Vegenaise.

Directions:

1. Peel grapefruits, removing all of the white pith.

2. Work over a large bowl to catch any juice. Remove the membrane from the outside of each segment and discard. Place fruit in the bowl with juice. Add onion and toss well.

3. Arrange lettuce leaves on a platter, then artfully arrange slices of avocado on top.

4. Spoon grapefruit and onion mixture onto the avocado slices. Garnish with arugula and a dollop of mayonnaise, then chill or serve.

The only commercial mayonnaise that we can recommend is Follow Your Heart (www.followyour-heart.com). Be sure to use the variety made with grapeseed oil.

Chunks of Chicken Salad

Salad:

4 to 5 cups free-range chicken, cooked, chopped into bite-size pieces

½ cup red onion, finely chopped

1 cup jicama, diced

1 cup red bell pepper, diced

1 cup cucumber, sliced thin

1 cup cilantro or parsley, coarsely chopped

Romaine lettuce leaves

Dressing:

¾ cup of Lemon Rosemary Garlic Dressing (page 99)

Directions:

1. Toss all ingredients together in a large bowl.

2. Arrange lettuce leaves on a plate and top with a large scoop of salad.

The classic chicken salad is made with a lot of greasy mayonnaise that contains trans fats. Our Chunks of Chicken Salad can be made with our Classic Homemade Mayonnaise (page 94), or you can use a simple olive oil dressing or the Lemon Rosemary Garlic dressing as we are suggesting here. There are also a number to choose from in the Salad Dressings section.

Body Ecology's Version of a Classic Chopped Salad

Salad:

1 large head romaine lettuce, chopped (*see sidebar*)

1 small red bell pepper, diced

1 cup jicama, peeled, diced

1 medium cucumber, peeled, seeded, diced

1 cup sliced arugula, tough stems removed

1 cup thinly sliced napa, savoy or other soft cabbage, parboiled, chilled, chopped (*see sidebar*)

2 cups celery, diced

3 cups turkey breast, diced

2 tablespoons scallions, chopped

Dressing:

1 teaspoon garlic, minced

2 teaspoons shallots, minced

3 tablespoons fresh parsley, minced

⅛ cup balsamic vinegar

⅛ cup raw, organic apple cider vinegar

1 teaspoon Dijon mustard

1 ⅓ cups organic, unfiltered olive oil

½ teaspoon Celtic sea salt, or more to taste

Directions:

1. Toss all salad ingredients in a large bowl and chill.

2. Whisk dressing ingredients in a small bowl and chill for at least one hour.

3. Toss dressing with salad ingredients just before serving in large individual salad bowls.

How To Cut Lettuce for a Perfect Chopped Salad

1. Wash and spin dry romaine lettuce leaves.

2. Stack leaves and cut lengthwise into strips about ½ inch wide.

3. Turn the stack and chop leaves into ½-inch dice.

Turkey Salad

Salad:

4 cups cooked turkey, chopped into bite-size pieces

1 cup red onion, finely chopped

1 cup celery, finely chopped

1 cup red bell pepper, finely chopped

1 teaspoon Celtic sea salt

Mixed field greens

Vinaigrette:

½ cup raw, organic apple cider vinegar

½ cup lemon juice, freshly squeezed

4 tablespoons Dijon mustard

1 teaspoon dried rosemary

½ teaspoon Celtic sea salt

1 cup organic, unfiltered olive oil

1 teaspoon xanthan gum (optional)

Directions:

1. Blend vinaigrette ingredients in a small bowl. Slowly whisk in olive oil and xanthan gum, if using.

2. Toss all ingredients with the vinaigrette in a medium-sized bowl. Refrigerate several hours to marinate flavors. Serve over mixed field greens.

Grilled Ribeye Salad

Salad:

1 teaspoon fresh ginger

16 ounces of ribeye steak, trimmed

16 scallions, white parts only

1 red bell pepper, quartered, seeded

8 cups torn salad greens

Celtic sea salt, to taste

Dressing:

1 garlic clove

2 tablespoons wheat-free tamari

2 tablespoons raw, organic apple cider vinegar

2 teaspoons olive oil

1 teaspoon Lakanto

Directions:

1. Preheat grill to high.

2. Combine garlic, tamari, vinegar, oil, Lakanto, and ginger. Blend until smooth. Set aside.

3. Season both sides of ribeye with sea salt.

4. Grill steak, scallions and bell peppers for 5 minutes. (Allow steaks to develop a char.) Turn. Cook 3 to 5 minutes longer.

5. Let steak rest for 5 minutes. Thinly slice meat against the grain.

6. While steak is resting, halve the scallions and cut peppers into strips.

7. Toss greens with dressing and arrange sliced steak on top. Garnish with the scallions and peppers.

Tuna Niçoise Salad ■ ■ ■ ■ ■ ■

Salad:

2 cans Ventresca tuna, drained, diced

1 medium cucumber, seeded, diced small

1 small red bell pepper, diced

2 stalks celery, diced

½ pound green beans, cooked, cut into 1-inch pieces

¼ cup red onion, diced small

½ cup fresh corn kernels cut off cob

½ cup parsley or cilantro

1 bunch of Romaine lettuce hearts, coarsely chopped

4 hard-boiled eggs, peeled, cut into quarters or eighths

Herbamare, to taste

Dressing:

4 tablespoons organic, unfiltered olive oil

2 tablespoons raw, organic apple cider vinegar

2 tablespoons balsamic vinegar

1 clove of garlic, minced, or use garlic press

1 anchovy fillet, minced

½ teaspoon Celtic sea salt

Directions:

1. Sprinkle diced cucumber and bell peppers with sea salt and put into a colander. Weight with a small saucer to assist with draining excess liquid.

2. Whisk together the ingredients for the salad dressing in a bowl.

3. Toss some of salad dressing with the romaine lettuce and place in 4 individual salad bowls.

4. Combine tuna, cucumber, red pepper, celery, green beans, red onion, corn, parsley or cilantro with the remaining salad dressing and let marinate for 15 minutes or longer.

5. Arrange the tuna mixture on top of the romaine.

6. Garnish with egg wedges and a sprinkle of Herbamare. Drizzle with more dressing or olive oil, if desired.

While the traditional Niçoise recipe calls for potatoes, we've left them out of our recipe because they aren't ideal for proper food combining. If you must add them, then do.

We really like Ventresca Tuna from Vital Choice, but you can use chicken or any proteins, such as lamb, beef, turkey, turkey sausage, canned salmon, etc.

Salmon Salad with Dill Vinaigrette ■ ■ ■ ■ ■ ■

Salad:

2 six-ounce cans boneless skinless pink salmon

1 cup red bell pepper, chopped

1 cup cucumber, chopped

½ cup red onion, chopped

¼ teaspoon Celtic sea salt

Vinaigrette:

1 tablespoon organic, unfiltered olive oil

2 tablespoons fresh dill, chopped

¼ cup lemon juice, freshly squeezed

⅛ teaspoon Celtic sea salt

Directions:

1. Flake salmon with a fork into a large bowl. Add the next 4 ingredients and stir gently to combine.

2. Combine the dill, lemon juice, and sea salt in a medium bowl and slowly whisk in olive oil.

3. Toss salad with the vinaigrette immediately before serving. Use a slotted spoon to serve.

Quinoa Curry Salad with Fermented Coconut and Turmeric Dressing

■ ■ ■ ■ ■ ■

Salad:

4 cups cooked quinoa, chilled

4 English cucumbers, chopped

1 bunch cilantro, chopped

1 red bell pepper, chopped

Dressing:

1 cup fermented young coconut meat

1 to 2 limes, juiced

½ to 1 teaspoon curry powder

½ to 1 teaspoon turmeric

½ to 1 teaspoon cumin

½ to 1 garlic clove

Cayenne pepper, to taste

Celtic sea salt, to taste

Directions:

1. Mix cooled quinoa with cucumbers, cilantro and bell pepper in a large bowl.

2. Blend all dressing ingredients in a high speed blender and pour over salad. Mix gently.

3. Refrigerate for an hour before serving. Garnish with a few cilantro leaves and a sprinkle of turmeric.

Have you been looking for new, delicious ways to incorporate fermented proteins into your diet? This recipe uses raw, vegan, fermented young coconut meat, an easy-to-digest source of protein. Curry, turmeric and cumin are all anti-inflammatory herbs. Turmeric, a well-known Ayurvedic liver support herb, is also a superb antioxidant. Enjoy with a serving of cultured beets! This recipe makes enough for a group, or for you to have delicious leftovers.

Warm Quinoa and Veggie Salad

■ ■ ■ ■ ■ ■

Salad:

2 cups quinoa or millet, cooked

⅔ cup frozen peas

⅔ cup frozen or fresh corn

⅔ cup red bell peppers, finely diced

1 bunch scallions or 1 red onion, finely chopped

Dressing:

1 cup or more Oil-free Rosemary Dressing (page 98) or a vinaigrette of your choice.

Directions:

1. Steam carrots, peas, and corn 4 to 6 minutes. The vegetables should be cooked but still slightly firm.

2. Combine all ingredients in a large bowl and serve.

Quinoa Tabouli Salad

Salad:

1 cup quinoa, cooked and chilled
  (*see sidebar*)

¼ cup organic, unfiltered olive oil

¼ cup lemon juice, freshly squeezed

2 cups fresh parsley, chopped

1 cup scallions, finely chopped

¼ cup fresh mint, chopped

2 red bell peppers, diced small

1 cucumber, peeled, seeded, chopped

1 teaspoon Celtic sea salt

Directions:

1. Pour quinoa into large mixing bowl. Add oil and lemon juice and mix lightly. Add parsley, red bell pepper, scallions, cucumber, and mint. Toss to mix.

2. Cover. Chill for at least one hour or overnight. Add sea salt. Mix lightly and serve.

Quinoa and Cilantro Salad with Lemon and Garlic

Salad:

1 cup of quinoa, cooked and chilled
  (*see sidebar*)

1 tablespoon of Celtic sea salt

1 cup filtered water

½ bunch cilantro, washed, spun dry, chopped into bite-size pieces

½ cup corn, chopped

½ cup parsley, minced

Dressing:

2 garlic cloves, minced

¼ cup lemon juice, freshly squeezed

2 tablespoons organic, unfiltered olive oil

Directions:

1. Pour quinoa into a large salad bowl and fluff again with fork.

2. Combine garlic, lemon juice, olive oil, and sea salt. Pour over quinoa and toss well.

3. Add cilantro, corn and parsley and toss gently. Serve at room temperature or chilled.

Our Secret to Fluffy and Low-Oxalate Grain-like Seeds

The secret to creating a nice, fluffy quinoa and millet to use in salad recipes is to cook these grain-like seeds just as you would pasta. Take a tall stockpot of water, add 1 to 2 teaspoons of sea salt, and bring water to a rolling boil. Then drop in the quinoa or millet and cook it about 12 to 15 minutes. Millet usually needs a few minutes longer. Drain, catching the quinoa or millet in a fine-mesh colander, then fluff with a fork. As an added bonus, this is also the Body Ecology secret technique to removing oxalates!

Millet Tabouli Salad with Garlic-Mint Dressing ■ ■ ■ ■ ■

Salad:

2 cups millet, cooked and chilled (*see sidebar on previous page*)

1 cup fresh dill, chopped

1 cup fresh parsley, chopped

1 cup fresh mint, chopped

½ cup fresh chives, chopped

1 cup red bell peppers, chopped

1 cup zucchini, steamed, cooled

1 teaspoon raw, organic apple cider vinegar

Dressing:

¼ to ⅓ cup lemon juice, freshly squeezed, or to taste

½ cup organic, unfiltered olive oil or flax oil

2 garlic cloves, minced

4 tablespoons fresh mint leaves, minced

Celtic sea salt, to taste

Directions:

1. Pour millet into a large mixing bowl then toss in chopped herbs, vegetables and vinegar.

2. Blend lemon juice, mint, and garlic in a high-speed blender. Slowly add oil until emulsified.

3. Toss salad with dressing and serve.

Fresh herbs are abundant during the summer season. Enjoy this delicious millet salad with herbs like mint and chives as a side dish or even a main course. It packs really well for summertime picnics and cookouts. The dressing is great on other salads, too!

Notes

Notes

Notes

Salad Dressings ■ ■ ■ ■ ■ ■

I'm sure you've heard the saying that an apple a day keeps the doctor away. Here at Body Ecology a salad plays that role, and it's the dressing that truly makes the salad! And there's an art to making a salad dressing. Made properly, dressings are not only delicious but allow you to incorporate high quality, healing, virgin (or unrefined) oils. A Body Ecology dressing always includes apple cider vinegar or lemon juice. Both are alkaline and cleansing. And don't forget about tasty olive oil! In the Body Ecology kitchen, like some collect fine wines, we delight in collecting olive oils from different estates. The flavors and lovely aromas of olive oil can be delicate and buttery, fruity and fragrant, mild and peppery, to green and grassy. They not only stimulate your taste buds and inspire you to tour the groves of Italy, Spain and California, but they're also heart-healthy and reduce inflammation.

The Importance of Organic, Unrefined Oils

I used to think that "cold-pressed" or "expeller-pressed" oils sold in health-food stores were healthy. But years ago I started working with an enzyme therapist who tested urine samples and found that people simply were not digesting these fats. Why? The problem sent me on an intensive search for an answer. I learned that the liver, a key digestive organ, must have totally unrefined oils. It just wasn't created to process the man-made, refined oils that Americans have been eating for generations. Even if you find them in a health-food store and even if they are labeled "cold-pressed," they are still bleached, deodorized, and refined. They lack essential fatty acids, color, and flavor. Organic, unrefined oils, however, provide you with essential fatty acids.

You may have noticed that when you eat oils, you become bloated and have gas in your intestines. If so, try keeping all fats and oils to a minimum until your inner ecosystem is well established. Beneficial microbiota play an important role in digesting fats and oils, so as you begin to eat and drink fermented foods and liquids, your ability to digest fats and oils should improve significantly. Because fats are digested in your small intestine

Choosing Apple Cider Vinegar

Apple cider vinegar is manufactured by several different companies. Look for unfiltered vinegar packaged in light-proof or opaque containers. Good packaging prevents photo oxidation and ensures the integrity of the product. The label should tell you that the vinegar is raw, unpasteurized, and contains the "mother," and the more of it, the better.

Rich in potassium and alkaline-forming, apple cider vinegar acts as an antidote when you've had too much salt or sugar. It's delicious in The Body Ecology Diet Salad Dressing (page 94), and you can use it to substitute for other vinegars in various recipes, even Classic Homemade Mayonnaise (page 94).

you will definitely notice improved digestion if you also take a pancreatic enzyme. (Body Ecology offers one called ASSIST SI.) Our goal is to help you create a thriving inner ecosystem, so that you can eat and enjoy oils that really are essential for creating ideal health.

Organic, unrefined seed and nut oils are raw and cold-pressed. They are processed with an amazing amount of care. Organic seeds and nuts such as flax, pumpkin, evening primrose, borage, and walnuts are gently pressed to release their oils. The oils are never exposed to light or oxygen, and have no preservatives. They are packaged in light-proof bottles and are each stamped with an expiration date. Because they are stronger and more flavorful than the oils you grew up eating, they may take some getting used to. Most people love their rich taste and would never go back to refined, "plasticized" oils.

Flax seed oil is an excellent source of omega-3 fatty acid, but fish oil is a more reliable one. We don't often use fish oil in a salad dressing but some brands can work without a fishy taste, so try them! We tend to be very deficient in omega-3 fatty acids today. Omega-3 is easily destroyed by heat, so we never cook with it. Unrefined canola oil (made from rapeseed) is another source of omega-3s but we do not use it because of its strong, bitter flavor. The commercial canola oil you see everywhere these days has no color or flavor, so you know it is refined.

Extra-virgin olive oil enjoys high praise among nutritionists, and many people report that they digest it well. Extra virgin means it's unrefined. Many stores sell high-quality, extra-virgin, unrefined olive oil. Olive oil has only small amounts of omega-3 essential fatty acids and has much more omega-9, which has heart protective properties. You can use it generously on The Body Ecology Diet.

If you really want to know which oils are best for your unique body, take a nutritional genomics test from a company such as Pathway Genomics (www.pathwaygenomics.com), Fitgenes (www.fitgenes.com), or smartDNA (www.smart.dna.com.au/public). Interestingly, some people find olive oil highly beneficial to their genes and others find it is only neutral. A small subset of people does not seem to do well on olive oil at all and as the science around nutritional genomics becomes better understood we should soon know why.

No-Oil Dressings for Better Digestion

Without a healthy inner ecosystem, many people have trouble digesting fats and oils. And sometimes you may want or need to avoid oils but still want to enjoy fresh salads with your meals. These times include:

1. When you're just beginning The Diet and your digestion is not yet strong enough to handle oils. Remember though, once you've added fermented foods into your diet you should be able to more easily absorb the important fatty acids that the good fats and oils offer. Digestive enzymes like pancreatin and ox bile may also become valuable, fat-digesting tools.

2. If you are giving your liver and gallbladder a rest with a cleansing program that eliminates oils.

Both of these situations call for a no-oil dressing. You've probably seen such dressings in stores, but you may not know how to make one. The solution is a gel fiber called xanthan gum. Simply remove the oil from any favorite dressing recipe, substitute an equal amount of water and a little xanthan gum to thicken, and add a variety of herbs and seasonings! Once you become familiar with xanthan gum, you'll soon be creating dressings of your own. Our recipes are simply guidelines to stimulate your own creativity.

Mixing It Up!

Nearly all of our dressings can be made with a countertop blender, a handheld blender, or a food processor. Depending on the ingredients, a large wire whisk or a shaker jar will work too. Whichever appliance or method you choose, the goal is to create an emulsion. Emulsification is the vigorous blending of liquids that would not ordinarily mix well (like water and oil) into droplets so small that they will remain separated for an extended time. Unless otherwise noted, you can use this method to create the recipes in this section: Blend salad dressing ingredients until smooth and then slowly add the oil in a stream until it's incorporated. Dressings made by whisking will be less creamy and those made using a machine will be more so. Simple!

Oil-free dressings can be very handy when you want to have a protein meal and a salad. Remember that large amounts of oil (a tuna-fish salad with mayo, for example) inhibit the secretion of hydrochloric acid (HCl) in the stomach. You need both HCl and pepsin to digest protein. A tuna-fish salad made with a no-oil or low-oil dressing can taste fabulous. Now you can create egg, tuna, and chicken-salad masterpieces, or serve a pumpkin seed, or sunflower seed paté.

Dressings made with no oil, or only the highest-quality unrefined oils, are beginning to play a key role in helping us become healthier. As more of us eliminate poor-quality fats and oils from our diets, many diseases we suffer from today will simply go away.

The Body Ecology Diet Salad Dressing

■ ■ ■ ■ ■ ■

Ingredients for ¼ Cup:

2 tablespoons organic, unrefined olive oil

1 tablespoon flax seed oil or a flax seed/evening primrose oil blend

1 tablespoon raw, organic apple cider vinegar or lemon juice

¼ to ½ teaspoon Celtic sea salt and/or Herbamare to taste

¼ teaspoon xanthan gum, if desired

This dressing is a Body Ecology favorite because it is so versatile! You can experiment with small amounts of flavorful oils, such as walnut or roasted pumpkin seed oil, a wonderful mustard, or your favorite herbs. For even more variety, try Sea Seasonings Dulse or Dulse with Garlic, a dash of homemade mayonnaise (or Follow Your Heart Vegenaise made with grapeseed oil), a pinch of cayenne pepper, or ½ teaspoon EcoBloom (a prebiotic that encourages the growth of friendly bifidus microorganisms).

If you're using xanthan gum as a thickening agent, blend it in just after adding the oil.

This recipe is easily doubled or even quadrupled. Refrigerate any leftovers for up to 10 days.

Classic Homemade Mayonnaise

■ ■ ■ ■ ■ ■

Ingredients:

2 fertile or organic free-range egg yolks

2 tablespoons raw, organic apple cider vinegar

1 tablespoon lemon juice, freshly squeezed

½ teaspoon mustard

⅛ teaspoon cayenne pepper

2 teaspoons Celtic sea salt, or to taste

1 cup organic, unfiltered olive oil

Directions:

1. Combine egg yolks, vinegar, lemon juice, mustard, cayenne pepper, sea salt, and ¼ cup olive oil in a blender. Blend for 30 to 45 seconds.

2. With blender running low, drizzle remaining oil in a thin stream until mixture is thick. Scrape into a glass jar with a screw top, and it will keep safely in your refrigerator 7 to 14 days.

Additional options can include: garlic powder, a dash of white pepper, ¼ teaspoon mustard powder, and herbs (chervil, tarragon, dill, oregano, basil, cumin, coriander, curry, paprika). Cayenne pepper and/or lime juice gives the mayonnaise a nice flavor for topping aspics or for mixing into salads. Mayonnaise can be sweetened with a few drops of stevia liquid concentrate. Instead of vinegar, try 2 teaspoons finely grated lemon peel, 2 teaspoons fresh lemon juice, and 1 teaspoon fresh mustard.

Almond Mayonnaise

■ ■ ■ ■ ■ ■

Ingredients for ¼ Cup:

½ cup raw almonds, soaked for at least 8 hours

½ to ¾ cup filtered water

¼ teaspoon garlic powder

¾ teaspoon Celtic sea salt

1 cup organic, unrefined flax or pumpkin seed oil

3 tablespoons lemon juice

½ teaspoon raw, organic apple cider vinegar

Directions:

1. Cover almonds with boiling water. Allow to cool slightly and then slip off skins.

2. Place almonds in blender or food processor and grind to a fine powder. Add half the water, garlic powder and salt. Blend well. Add the remaining water and process until creamy.

3. Drizzle the oil into the mixture and process until thick. Add lemon juice and vinegar and process for 1 minute to allow mixture to thicken.

4. Store mayonnaise in a screw-top jar in refrigerator for 10 days to 2 weeks.

This recipe appears in The Body Ecology Diet *and is adapted from* The American Vegetarian Cookbook *from the Fit for Life Kitchen, a masterpiece by Marilyn Diamond. While Marilyn has included it in her book as an alternative to mayonnaise made with eggs, we think it's an excellent party dip or snack food when served with raw vegetables.*

If you have trouble digesting oil, eliminate the oil completely and increase the water.

Apple Cider Vinaigrette

■ ■ ■ ■ ■ ■

Ingredients:

1 shallot

½ cup fresh basil leaves

½ cup fresh tarragon

1 tablespoon Dijon mustard

¼ cup raw, organic apple cider vinegar

¾ cup organic, unfiltered olive oil

1 drop Body Ecology stevia liquid concentrate

This dressing can be modified countless ways. By changing the mustard, the flavor of the vinegar, or by adding herbs you can create different recipes to suit your particular tastes.

Creamy Garlic Dressing

■ ■ ■ ■ ■ ■

Ingredients:

¼ cup fresh lemon juice

¼ cup wheat-free tamari

8 garlic cloves, peeled

1 three-inch piece ginger, peeled

1¼ cups organic, unfiltered olive oil

Dyan's Delicious Salad Dressing ■ ■ ■ ■ ■ ■

Ingredients:

⅔ cup organic, unfiltered olive oil

⅓ cup flaxseed oil

¼ cup raw, organic apple cider vinegar

2 tablespoons roasted pumpkin seed oil

2 tablespoons dulse

1 teaspoon garlic powder

Celtic sea salt or Herbamare, to taste

Pinch of cayenne pepper

Ginger Dressing ■ ■ ■ ■ ■ ■

Ingredients:

2 tablespoons raw, organic apple cider
   vinegar

1 tablespoon wheat-free tamari

1 tablespoon organic, unfiltered olive oil

1 teaspoon ginger, freshly grated

1 tablespoon cilantro, chopped

¼ teaspoon cayenne pepper

½ teaspoon sesame oil

Celtic sea salt, to taste

Milk Kefir Dressing ■ ■ ■ ■ ■ ■

Ingredients:

½ ripe avocado, peeled

¾ cup fermented milk kefir

4 tablespoons lemon juice, freshly squeezed

2 tablespoons fresh tarragon leaves,
   coarsely chopped

1 scallion, white and green parts, coarsely
   chopped

½ teaspoon Celtic sea salt

Pinch of Herbamare

¼ teaspoon freshly ground black pepper

Because this dressing contains dairy, it is not recommended in Stage 1 of The Body Ecology Diet. You can refrigerate leftover dressing for 2 to 3 days in an airtight container.

Lemon Herb Dressing ■ ■ ■ ■ ■ ■

Ingredients:

3 tablespoons organic, unfiltered olive oil

3 tablespoons walnut oil

1 teaspoon fresh thyme or ¼ teaspoon dry

2 tablespoons fresh oregano or
   ½ teaspoon dry

1 teaspoon lemon zest

Celtic sea salt, to taste

Pinch of cayenne pepper

Green Onion Dressing

Ingredients:

1 cup organic, unfiltered olive oil

½ cup Lakanto

¼ cup raw, organic apple cider vinegar

¼ teaspoon Celtic sea salt

5 or 6 green onions, chopped

Italian Dressing

Ingredients:

1 cup organic, unfiltered olive oil

½ cup raw, organic apple cider vinegar or fresh lemon juice

1 teaspoon Celtic sea salt, or to taste

⅛ teaspoon white pepper

½ teaspoon dry mustard

2 teaspoons Italian-blend seasoning

1 garlic clove, minced

Directions:

1. Combine all ingredients in a jar; cover tightly and shake vigorously.

2. Adjust seasonings to taste. Chill thoroughly.

Jeannine's Italian Dressing

Ingredients:

½ cup raw, organic apple cider vinegar

½ cup lemon juice, freshly squeezed

1½ cups filtered water

2 tablespoons minced garlic

2 tablespoons whole-grain mustard made with apple cider vinegar

2 tablespoons fresh parsley, finely chopped

2 teaspoons Celtic sea salt

2 tablespoons red pepper, finely chopped

¼ teaspoon each: dried oregano, basil, and thyme or 1 teaspoon Spice Hunter Italian Seasoning Blend

1 teaspoon xanthan gum

Directions:

1. Blend all ingredients except xanthan gum.

2. Add xanthan gum and blend or shake well. Refrigerate overnight.

Dairy-Free Tzatziki

■ ■ □ ■ ■ ■ ■

Ingredients:

2 cups fermented young coconut "pudding" or coconut kefir cheese (page 178)

3 garlic cloves

¼ cup freshly squeezed lemon juice

2 tablespoons fresh dill, chopped

½ cucumber, chopped

2 tablespoons organic, unfiltered olive oil

2 tablespoons pumpkinseed oil

2 tablespoons coconut oil

2 tablespoons walnut oil

Herbamare and/or sea salt to taste

Directions:

1. Combine the fermented coconut meat, garlic, lemon juice, dill and cucumber in a food processor. Blend until smooth.

2. Combine the oils in a bowl then process with the coconut-meat mixture until emulsified.

3. Season to taste with Herbamare and/or Celtic sea salt.

This is the Body Ecology version of the classic Greek favorite made with plain yogurt. If you are fine with dairy, you can also make it with fermented milk kefir (in Stage 2 only) instead of the fermented coconut pudding.

Surprisingly Delicious Super Spirulina and Seaweed Salad Dressing

■ ■ □ ■ ■ ■ ■

Ingredients:

4 tablespoons organic, unfiltered olive oil

2 tablespoons raw, organic apple cider vinegar

2 teaspoons Super Spirulina Plus™

1 teaspoon dulse flakes

1 teaspoon Celtic Sea Salt, or to taste

Garlic powder, to taste

Cayenne pepper, to taste

Oil-Free Rosemary Dressing

■ ■ □ ■ ■ ■ ■

Ingredients:

½ cup raw, organic apple cider vinegar

½ cup freshly squeezed lemon juice

1 cup filtered water

4 tablespoons mustard

1 teaspoon rosemary

½ teaspoon Celtic sea salt

1 teaspoon xanthan gum

Directions:

1. Blend first 6 ingredients, then add xanthan gum. Blend or shake well.

2. Refrigerate overnight. The dressing keeps up to a week.

This dressing is great on potato salad!

Lemon Rosemary Garlic Dressing ■ ■ ■ ■ ■ ■

Ingredients:

1 cup organic, unfiltered apple cider vinegar

1½ cups filtered water

½ cup lemon juice, freshly squeezed

2 tablespoons minced garlic

½ teaspoon celery seed

6 tablespoons red onion, diced

2 tablespoons red bell pepper, diced

1 teaspoon dill

2 tablespoons fresh parsley, minced

3 teaspoons Celtic sea salt

2 tablespoons dried rosemary, crushed *or* 4 tablespoons fresh rosemary, finely chopped

1 teaspoon xanthan gum

Directions:

1. Blend all ingredients except xanthan gum.

2. Add xanthan gum and blend or shake well. Refrigerate overnight.

Roasted Garlic Vinaigrette ■ ■ ■ ■ ■ ■

Ingredients:

2 whole bulbs garlic, roasted, skins removed

1/3 cup lemon juice, freshly squeezed

2 teaspoons organic, unfiltered olive oil

3 teaspoons pumpkinseed oil

3 tablespoons filtered water

¼ cup parsley, coarsely chopped

Celtic sea salt, to taste

Mint Garlic Dressing ■ ■ ■ ■ ■ ■

Ingredients:

¼ to 1/3 cup fresh lemon juice, to taste (start with less)

½ cup organic, unfiltered olive oil

2 garlic cloves, minced

1 tablespoon fresh mint leaves, minced

This dressing is great with Quinoa Tabouli Salad (page 85).

Mustard Vinaigrette ■ ■ ■ ■ ■ ■

Ingredients:

½ cup raw, organic apple cider vinegar

¼ cup organic, unfiltered olive oil

¼ cup walnut oil

2 tablespoons coarse mustard

1 teaspoon dried basil

Celtic sea salt, to taste

Walnut oil is a nice substitute for olive oil in this recipe!

Champagne Vinaigrette

■ ▪ ■ ■ ■ ■

Ingredients:

¼ teaspoon yellow mustard

2 egg yolks

½ cup extra-virgin olive oil

3 tablespoons coconut vinegar

Juice of 1 lemon

1 teaspoon Celtic Sea Salt or Herbamare

Directions:

1. In a bowl, whisk together the mustard and the egg yolk.

2. Whisk in the vinegar then slowly drizzle in the olive oil.

3. Season with salt or Herbamare to taste.

Tangy Vinaigrette

■ ▪ ■ ■ ■ ■

Ingredients:

2 tablespoons raw, organic apple cider vinegar

3 tablespoons organic, unfiltered olive oil

3 tablespoons walnut oil

1 teaspoon fresh thyme

2 teaspoons oregano

1 teaspoon lemon zest

¼ teaspoon cayenne pepper

Celtic sea salt, to taste

Directions:

After blending, allow the flavors to marry for 4 hours in the refrigerator before tossing with salad and serving.

Watercress Dressing

■ ▪ ■ ■ ■ ■

Ingredients:

2 tablespoons lemon juice, freshly squeezed

1 tablespoon raw, organic apple cider vinegar

¼ cup organic, unfiltered olive oil

½ teaspoon dried tarragon

Celtic sea salt, to taste

1 bunch watercress, finely chopped

Directions:

After blending the first 5 ingredients, stir in the finely chopped watercress by hand.

Notes

Notes

Notes

Sauces

■ ■ ■ ■ ■

Learning to whip up a tasty sauce in minutes is the sign of a skillful chef. You'll convince even the pickiest eaters in your family to eat grain-like seeds and protein dishes when they're served with a simple sauce. All of the recipes here are very easy to make but be creative and don't limit your imagination. Try to keep a sauce in your refrigerator at all times and one way to do that is to keep a creamy soup on hand.

Soups, especially creamy soups, such as Broccoli and Fresh Fennel (page 54) and our Creamy Dilled Cauliflower (page 56) make wonderful sauces. You can jazz up the dilled cauliflower soup by adding shiitake mushrooms and use it as a base in many recipes, even some of your old family favorites.

Reserve a few cups of the Oil-Free Carrot and Cauliflower Soup (page 55), add a tablespoon (or more) of whole-grain mustard, and serve it as a delicious new sauce. It's very good over steamed vegetables!

Brett's Dipping Sauce

■ ■ ■ ■ ■ ■ ■

Ingredients:

2 garlic cloves, minced

1 bunch of scallions, greens only, roughly chopped

2 ounces fresh shiitake mushrooms, de-stemmed, minced

1 cup homemade vegetable stock (page 57)

½ cup wheat-free tamari

3 tablespoons roasted pumpkinseed oil

Celtic sea salt, to taste

Directions:

1. Combine garlic, scallions, mushrooms and stock in a small saucepan. Slowly bring mixture to a simmer. Remove from heat. Cool for about 5 minutes.

2. Add tamari and purée the mixture in a food processor or blender.

3. Pour through a fine sieve or cheesecloth into a bowl. Discard pulp. Gently stir in pumpkinseed oil.

*This sauce has many uses. Try it as a basting liquid for chicken or when grilling fish or shrimp, or as the name suggests, use as a dipping sauce for oven-roasted veggies. It's also quite delicious poured on top of anything, especially grain-like seeds (quinoa, millet and buckwheat). **TIP:** Do not reheat sauce over high heat after you add the oil. Heating pumpkinseed oil will destroy its healing properties.*

Hot Sauce

■ ■ ■ ■ ■ ■ ■

Ingredients:

1 teaspoon jalapeño pepper, stemmed, seeded

¼ cup garlic, minced

5 tablespoons filtered water

1 cup fresh cilantro

1 teaspoon Celtic sea salt

1 teaspoon cumin

Directions:

1. Blend the jalapeño pepper and garlic in a food processor until it forms a paste.

2. Add water, cilantro, salt and cumin. Process for 30 seconds. Store in refrigerator for up to 2 weeks.

Cranberry Ginger Sauce

■ ■ ■ ■ ■ ■ ■

Ingredients:

8 ounces fresh cranberries

1 tablespoon fresh ginger, peeled, finely chopped

1 tablespoon lemon zest

2 cups filtered water

¼ teaspoon Body Ecology's stevia liquid concentrate

1 to 2 tablespoons vanilla extract

½ cup pecans or walnuts, soaked for at least 8 hours, coarsely chopped, then roasted in a dry skillet

Directions:

1. Bring cranberries and ginger to boil in a small saucepan. Cover and simmer until berries are slightly soft. Drain, reserving liquid.

2. Add remaining ingredients to the cranberries, adjust sweetness as desired and chill.

This recipe is versatile! Make ambrosia by folding in young coconut kefir "cheese." You can add Body Ecology's stevia liquid concentrate to the reserved cranberry-ginger liquid and use it to flavor drinks like young coconut kefir or Cocobiotic and InnergyBiotic.

Cranberries are an acid fruit. They can be eaten alone on an empty stomach but they also combine with a protein fat. (Milk kefir, coconut kefir "cheese," avocado, nuts, and seeds are all examples of protein fats.) This sauce may be eaten with a protein meal, but not if your digestion is poor.

Corn Chutney

Ingredients:

3 tablespoons coconut oil or ghee

1 medium onion, chopped

6 ears corn, kernels removed

1 red bell pepper, diced

9 tablespoons raw, organic apple cider vinegar

1 teaspoon Body Ecology's stevia liquid concentrate

3 garlic cloves, minced

2 tablespoons ginger, grated

3 teaspoons chili powder

$\frac{1}{8}$ teaspoon cinnamon

$\frac{1}{8}$ teaspoon ground cloves

$\frac{1}{8}$ teaspoon nutmeg

$\frac{1}{4}$ to $\frac{1}{2}$ teaspoon curry powder

1 tablespoon arrowroot powder, dissolved in 2 tablespoons filtered water

Directions:

1. Sauté onions in the coconut oil or ghee. Add remaining ingredients to the sauté pan except arrowroot. Cook for 5 to 10 minutes.

2. Add arrowroot mixture and stir well. Simmer for 3 to 5 minutes. Serve warm or chilled

Presto Pesto with Pumpkin Seeds

Ingredients:

1 garlic clove

1 handful fresh, chopped cilantro

2 tablespoons fresh, chopped parsley

1 teaspoon pumpkin seed oil

1½ cups raw pumpkin seeds, soaked 8 hours

Celtic sea salt to taste

Dash of cayenne pepper

Splash of organic, unfiltered olive oil

Directions:

1. Blend all ingredients in a food processor. Pulse until creamy.

2. Chill before serving.

Once you get the hang of making your own healthy dips like this one, you'll never miss your old dressings and spreads! This pumpkin pesto is so versatile. Alternate your favorite herbs and spices for a new twist each time you prepare it. It's great as a spread for wraps. You can even add CocoBiotic and boost your intake of friendly microbiota!

Curried Cauliflower Sauce

Ingredients:

2 tablespoons coconut oil or ghee

1 large onion, chopped

2 garlic cloves, minced

1½ teaspoons ginger, grated

1 tablespoon curry powder, or to taste

¼ teaspoon cayenne pepper

1 cup filtered water

1 cauliflower head, chopped

Celtic sea salt or Herbamare, to taste

Freshly squeezed lemon juice, to taste

Directions:

1. Sauté onion, garlic, ginger, curry powder, and cayenne pepper in coconut oil or ghee until the onions are translucent.

2. Add cauliflower and filtered water to the sautéed vegetables. Simmer until tender. Add sea salt and lemon juice.

Easy Béarnaise Sauce

Ingredients:

1 egg

1 teaspoon raw, organic apple cider vinegar

1 teaspoon mustard

1 tablespoon freshly squeezed lemon juice

½ cup coconut oil or ghee

Celtic sea salt, to taste

Directions:

1. Combine all ingredients in a blender except coconut oil or ghee and process until smooth.

2. Warm the coconut oil or ghee in a small pot and slowly add it to the sauce.

Luscious Lemon Butter Sauce

Ingredients:

½ cup ghee

1 tablespoon coconut oil

2 medium onions, finely chopped, or
    2 small scallions, thinly sliced

1/3 cup freshly squeezed lemon juice

½ teaspoon dried tarragon or 1 tablespoon
    finely torn fresh tarragon

½ teaspoon dried basil or 1 tablespoon
    finely chopped fresh basil

Directions:

Heat ghee and coconut oil in a small skillet. Add onions or scallions and sauté until soft. Add remaining ingredients, and simmer 10 minutes. Serve warm.

To vary the flavor, you can replace the tarragon and basil with ½ teaspoon of dried dill or 1 tablespoon of fresh dill.

Annmarie's Gingery Carrot Sauce ■ ■ ■ ■ ■ ■ ■

Ingredients:

1 tablespoon coconut oil or ghee

20 to 25 small carrots, chopped

2 large onions, diced

3 garlic cloves, minced

2½ stalks celery, chopped

1 small red bell pepper, chopped

Vegetable stock or filtered water

2½ teaspoons Celtic sea salt or Herbamare

1 tablespoon Italian seasoning

2 teaspoons garlic powder

Ginger juice, to taste

Directions:

1. Sauté carrots and onions in coconut oil or ghee. Add celery and red bell pepper and continue to sauté. Add vegetable stock or filtered water to cover, and sea salt or Herbamare. Pressure cook for 15 minutes or simmer until very soft.

2. Transfer mixture to a blender and purée. Add Italian seasoning, garlic powder, ginger juice and enough water to create the right consistency for a sauce.

3. Return to pan and simmer 10 to 15 minutes. Season to taste.

Our thanks to Annmarie Butera for this tasty recipe!

To make ginger juice, grate the ginger, then pick up a handful and squeeze the juice into small measuring cup.

For even more flavor, you can add a pinch of cumin, coriander, or cardamom to the carrots as they sauté.

Pesto ■ ■ ■ ■ ■ ■ ■

Ingredients:

3 to 4 cups fresh basil

¾ cup organic, unrefined olive oil or pumpkin seed oil

1 teaspoon Celtic sea salt

Zest of 1 lemon

1 lemon, juiced

3 to 4 garlic cloves

½ cup flat-leaf parsley

1 tablespoon lecithin

Directions:

1. Purée ingredients in a blender until very smooth.

2. Serve over noodles, grains, red potatoes, a salad, or a platter of vegetables.

Mock Tomato Sauce

Ingredients:

1 small red beet, sliced

6 cups of water

3 tablespoons coconut oil or ghee

4 cups red onion, diced

3 tablespoons garlic, finely chopped

3 tablespoons Spice Hunter pizza herb
    seasoning

1 medium zucchini, diced

2 medium butternut squashes

2 tablespoons of Celtic sea salt

6 cups filtered water

1 cup raw, organic apple cider vinegar

Directions:

1. Bring 2 cups filtered water to a boil. Add beet slices and simmer 30 minutes. Reserve broth, discard beets.

2. Sauté onions and garlic in oil or ghee until golden. Add pizza seasoning and zucchini and continue to sauté on low heat for 5 minutes. Remove from heat.

3. Preheat oven to 400 degrees F.

4. Pierce butternut squashes in several places with a fork. Bake until very soft, approximately 1½ to 2 hours. Slice in half and let stand until cool enough to handle. Remove seeds. Scoop out squash and add to sautéed vegetables.

5. Add remaining 4 cups of water and beet stock and simmer another 10 minutes to marry the flavors.

6. Purée in batches in a blender or use an immersion blender. Adjust water and salt to desired thickness and flavor.

7. Let stand until room temperature and stir in apple cider vinegar.

We don't recommend tomatoes in large amounts in Stage 1 of The Body Ecology Diet, so we created this recipe for those who love tomato sauce. Adding apple cider vinegar at the end of cooking will more closely duplicate the acidic quality of a tomato sauce. The small amount of beet in this recipe is added merely for color and will not cause a problem with candida or blood sugar. This sauce is great over millet or buckwheat croquettes! Later, on special occasions you can use it on top of a gluten-free pizza crust. No one will even know the difference.

Body Ecology's Gluten-Free Gravy

Ingredients:

1 medium onion, thinly sliced

3 cups of shiitake mushrooms, thinly sliced

3 tablespoons coconut oil or ghee

2½ to 3 tablespoons amaranth flour

2 cups vegetable stock or filtered water

¼ teaspoon garlic, minced

1 teaspoon of Spice Hunter's many
  seasoning blends, such as Herbs de
  Provence or Deliciously Dill

Celtic sea salt or Herbamare, to taste

Directions:

1. Sauté onions and shiitake mushrooms slowly with 1 tablespoon of coconut oil or ghee in a small skillet until onions are just golden. Add garlic and cook for 1 minute. Remove mixture from skillet and set aside.

2. Heat the coconut oil or ghee in the same skillet and quickly stir in flour. Very slowly add vegetable stock or water, stirring constantly.

3. Add seasoning blend and return onions, mushrooms and garlic to skillet.

4. Add salt or Herbamare to taste.

This delicious recipe is greatly enhanced by the sautéed onions and shiitake mushrooms, which give the gravy that rich, umami taste! It's perfect for special occasions, such as Thanksgiving and other holidays when a traditional gravy is needed. You can also make the gravy without the onions and shiitakes if your meal is lighter or more casual.

Warm Fennel Compote

Ingredients:

2 medium bulbs fennel (about 2 pounds/
  5 cups), trimmed, minced

1½ tablespoons coconut oil or ghee

2 tablespoons vegetable stock

¼ teaspoon fennel seed

¾ teaspoon Celtic sea salt

White pepper, to taste

Directions:

1. Toss fennel with coconut oil or ghee in a medium saucepan. Add stock and seeds. Cover and cook over low heat, stirring only 2 or 3 times. Cook for 2 hours and 15 minutes or until fennel is easily mashed with a fork.

2. Mash into a chunky purée.

3. Season with sea salt and white pepper.

Ladle this fragrant compote onto a dinner plate and top with a fillet of your favorite white fish or salmon.

Notes

Notes

Vegetables

Non-Starchy Vegetables
Starchy Vegetables
Ocean Vegetables

Vegetables are Nature's gift of abundance. They are not only the most abundant foods on Earth; they're the most perfect foods nature has given us. They are rich in the vitamins and minerals your body needs to heal, and their colors, textures, and shapes add excitement to any meal. Whether your favorite veggies are from the land or the ocean, we've included recipes that are sure to please!

Keeping It Clean!

Cleaning your store-bought veggies is a must, but a simple rinsing isn't enough to remove pesticides or other residue. You can purchase a vegetable wash from your local health food store or you can make your own using apple cider vinegar. Here's how:

In a standard spray bottle mix equal parts of apple cider vinegar and water. Spray your fruits or vegetables and let them sit about 4 to 5 minutes, then rinse and dry. Larger amounts of produce like kale, Brussels sprouts or cabbage can be soaked in a bowl of water with an equal amount of apple cider vinegar for several minutes. Rinse before preparation or storage.

If you've purchased organic fruits and vegetables they don't need washing. A healthy "biofilm" will have formed on the surface that was created by the beneficial bacteria and yeast to protect the plant while it was growing. This biofilm contains beneficial bacteria that will help create a robust diversity of beneficial microbes in your digestive tract. The visible white layer of film on a plum, for example, is a biofilm.

Non-starchy vegetables form excellent combinations with just about every other food. They're alkalizing, full of vital nutrients and antioxidants, and are protective against all diseases, even cancer. Combine them with oil, butter, or ghee; animal protein or eggs; grains, grain-like seeds or nuts and seeds; or starchy veggies like acorn squash or red potatoes. Even sour fruits such as lemons or limes go well with non-starchy vegetables. Basically, they should be eaten at every meal including breakfast!

Swiss Chard with Lemon   ■ ■ ■ ■ ■ ■ ■

Ingredients:

2 pounds Swiss chard

1 tablespoon coconut oil or ghee

½ teaspoon cumin

2 garlic cloves, chopped

½ lemon, sliced thin, then cut in half moons

¼ cup vegetable stock (page 57) or
    filtered water

Body Ecology's stevia liquid concentrate,
    to taste

Celtic sea salt, to taste

Directions:

1. Wash chard thoroughly, remove stems from leaves. If using stems, finely chop them.

2. Heat coconut oil or ghee in a deep sauté pan over medium heat. Add cumin seeds and cook, stirring, for 1 minute. Add garlic and chard stems, and cook 3 minutes. Stir in lemon slices.

3. Add half of the chard leaves and allow them to wilt before adding the other half. Add water or vegetable stock and sea salt and cook 1 to 2 minutes. Remove from heat. Stir in 1 to 3 drops of stevia liquid concentrate and sea salt to taste.

Broccoli and Sweet Pepper Sauté   ■ ■ ■ ■ ■ ■ ■

Ingredients:

2 pounds broccoli florets

2 tablespoons coconut oil or ghee

½ sweet onion, chopped

1 red bell pepper, seeded, cut into strips

Directions:

1. Lightly steam broccoli florets and set aside.

2. Sauté onions in coconut oil or ghee for about 5 to 7 minutes, or until golden around the edges.

3. Add pepper strips and sauté for an additional 3 to 5 minutes, or until peppers begin to soften.

4. Add broccoli, stir thoroughly, and cook until tender.

Cabbage and Collards

■ ■ ■ ■ ■ ■ ■

Ingredients:

5 tablespoons coconut or ghee

4 cups yellow onions, sliced

2 bunches collard greens, chopped

1 large head green cabbage, chopped

2 carrots, peeled and chopped into small chunks

2 cups water

Celtic sea salt, to taste

Directions:

1. Heat 4 tablespoons coconut or ghee over medium-low heat in a large sauté pan. Cook the onions, stirring occasionally, for approximately 45 minutes or until caramelized. Set aside.

2. Meanwhile, bring 2 cups of water to a boil in a medium stockpot. Add collard greens, carrots, onions and 1 tablespoon coconut oil or ghee. Cover, reduce heat, and simmer for 45 minutes, or until tender. Stir occasionally and add water if needed.

3. Stir in caramelized onions, sea salt and garlic powder. Cover and cook 5 to 10 more minutes until onions are heated through. Serve immediately.

Claire's Classy Carrots

■ ■ ■ ■ ■ ■ ■

Ingredients:

8 medium carrots, trimmed, cut on the diagonal into half-inch half-moons

Filtered water

2 tablespoons coconut oil or ghee

¼ to ½ teaspoon Frontier Herb orange flavoring or a few drops of essential therapeutic orange oil

Zest of one small orange

Body Ecology's stevia liquid concentrate, 4 to 6 drops or to taste

¼ cup fresh parsley, finely chopped

¼ teaspoon freshly squeezed lemon juice

Herbamare to taste

Directions:

1. Place carrots in a saucepan and cover with filtered water. Cook, covered, until just tender. Drain and set aside.

2. Lower heat and add coconut oil or ghee to the empty carrot pan. Add the orange flavoring, orange zest, and stevia to taste.

3. Gently toss the carrots in the orange mixture then turn off the heat. Add the parsley, Herbamare and lemon juice, toss again, and serve immediately.

Easy Collard Greens

■ ■ ■ ■ ■ ■ ■

Ingredients:

1 bunch collard greens, washed, leaving some water on the leaves

1 teaspoon Celtic sea salt

2 tablespoons olive oil

When you have a lot of things going on in the kitchen, it's nice to have this great fix-it and forget-it recipe! Because this is such a basic recipe, it is very easy to add your own special touches. Some people like onions and others a little hot pepper. Whatever you add, we are sure you'll have great results!

Directions:

1. Strip leaves from stems and set stems aside. Stack the leaves, roll, and slice cross-wise into half-inch strips.

2. Heat a large stockpot over medium-low heat. Add handfuls of greens while stirring; they will cook down quickly because of the residual water. Immediately sprinkle with salt and drizzle olive oil over the top of the greens but do not stir. Cover and turn the heat to a very low setting.

3. Cook 45 minutes, or until greens are very tender. When necessary, add just enough water to keep the greens moist.

Garlicky Green Beans

■ ■ ■ ■ ■ ■ ■

Ingredients:

2 pounds green beans, trimmed and cut in half

3 tablespoons olive oil, coconut oil or ghee

4 large garlic cloves, minced

Celtic sea salt, to taste

Directions:

1. Steam green beans. When tender, remove from heat, cover and set aside.

2. Melt olive oil, coconut oil or ghee in a sauté pan over medium-low heat. Sauté beans and garlic together and season with sea salt according to taste. Serve hot.

Roasted Asparagus

■ ■ ■ ■ ■ ■ ■

Ingredients:

1 pound asparagus, trimmed and peeled

2 tablespoons coconut oil or ghee

2 garlic cloves, minced

Celtic sea salt, to taste

Directions:

1. Preheat oven to 350 degrees.

2. Toss asparagus with garlic and coconut oil or ghee.

3. Arrange asparagus spears on a rimmed baking sheet and sprinkle with sea salt. Roast, turning occasionally, until asparagus is tender, approximately 25 minutes. Serve immediately.

Kale Sauté

■ ■ ■ ■ ■ ■ ■

Ingredients:

1 bunch kale, coarsely chopped

2 cups filtered water

2 teaspoons coconut oil or ghee

2 celery stalks, diced

1 garlic clove, minced

¼ cup red bell pepper, diced

Celtic sea salt, to taste

Raw, organic apple cider vinegar (optional)

Directions:

1. Strip kale leaves off the stalks. Discard stalks and coarsely chop leaves.

2. Bring filtered water to a boil, add kale, and cook over high heat for no more than 5 minutes. (If you overcook kale, it will go from sweet to bitter!) Drain kale and set aside.

3. Heat coconut oil or ghee in skillet over medium heat. Add celery and sauté 3 to 4 minutes. Add garlic and red pepper. Cover and cook for 2 minutes.

4. Stir in kale and cook until fully heated. Season with sea salt.

5. Just before eating, sprinkle with apple cider vinegar. Serve hot.

Red Slaw

■ ■ ■ ■ ■ ■ ■

Ingredients:

16 cups red cabbage, shredded, parboiled, chilled

4 cups carrots, sliced

1 cup green onion, chopped

2 tablespoons garlic cloves, minced

3 cups raw, organic apple cider vinegar

1 cup organic, unfiltered olive oil

Celtic sea salt to taste

Directions:

Mix all ingredients in a large bowl and toss thoroughly.

This makes a picnic-worthy quantity, but if your crowd is small you can easily halve the recipe.

Why Soak Nuts?

Nuts on The Body Ecology Diet are always presoaked for about 8 hours, to eliminate the phytic acid. Phytic acid is present in all grains, beans, nuts and seeds. It's called an "anti-nutrient" because it binds to minerals like zinc, magnesium and calcium preventing their absorption. Soaked nuts are an interesting flavor, but many people prefer to dehydrate them or toast them in an oven at a very low heat until they are a little crispy.

Dijon Roasted Brussels Sprouts   ■ ■ ■ ■ ■ ■ ■ ■

Ingredients:

¼ cup coconut oil or ghee

2 tablespoons creamy white mustard

2 tablespoons Lakanto sweetener

1 teaspoon wheat-free tamari

2 pounds Brussels sprouts, cored and
   quartered

Directions:

1. Preheat oven to 400 degrees.

2. Whisk first four ingredients together in medium-size bowl. Add Brussels sprouts and toss to coat.

3. Spread sprouts evenly on a baking sheet and roast until cores are tender, approximately 25 minutes. Stir sprouts and rotate pan halfway through cooking time. Serve hot.

Grilled Brussels Sprouts   ■ ■ ■ ■ ■ ■ ■ ■

Ingredients:

1 pound Brussels sprouts, trimmed at the
   root end, halved if large

1 tablespoon coconut oil or ghee

1 teaspoon fresh thyme, finely chopped

1 teaspoon raw, organic balsamic vinegar

½ teaspoon Celtic sea salt or Herbamare
   to taste

Zest of 1 lemon

When you grill Brussels sprouts until they are barely tender, they develop a lovely, subtle sweetness. Look for the smallest buds possible so that they cook quickly, or cut them in half.

Directions:

1. Prepare the grill for direct cooking over low heat (250 to 350 degrees) and preheat a cast iron grill pan.

2. In a medium bowl mix the coconut oil or ghee with the spices. Add the Brussels sprouts, and turn to coat evenly.

3. Spread the sprouts in a single layer on the grill pan. Grill until crisp-tender, about 10 to 15 minutes. Turn the sprouts several times, keeping the lid on the grill closed as much as possible.

4. Transfer to a serving bowl and add the lemon zest and balsamic vinegar. Toss to coat evenly. Season with sea salt or Herbamare. Serve warm.

Sautéed Kale with Garlic   ■ ■ ■ ■ ■ ■ ■ ■

Ingredients:

2 tablespoons olive oil, coconut oil, or ghee

1 large bunch of kale, washed, leaving water
   on the leaves, coarsely chopped

3 to 4 garlic cloves, coarsely chopped

Celtic sea salt, to taste

Directions:

1. Place chopped kale in large mixing bowl and knead with hands to break up fibers in kale.

2. Heat olive oil, coconut oil, or ghee in large skillet. Add kale, garlic and sea salt and sauté over low heat until kale wilts. Reduce heat as much as possible, cover skillet, and continue to let kale "sweat" until tender, approximately 35 to 45 minutes. Serve hot.

Roasted Cauliflower and Brussels Sprouts ■ ■ ▪ ■ ■ ■ ■

Ingredients:

2 tablespoons coconut oil or ghee

1 medium head of cauliflower, cut into small ½-1 inch florets

2 cups Brussels sprouts, trimmed and halved lengthwise

3 garlic cloves, minced

½ to 1 teaspoon dried rosemary

½ to 1 teaspoon Celtic sea salt

This recipe looks beautiful on the plate and has a rich, caramelized flavor!

Directions:

1. Preheat oven to 450 degrees.

2. Steam cauliflower and Brussels sprouts for 4 to 6 minutes. Place cauliflower and Brussels sprouts in a large bowl, let cool. Drizzle coconut oil or ghee on top, and then add garlic, rosemary and sea salt.

3. Spread vegetables in single layer on an oiled roasting pan. Roast until vegetables are tender and crispy on the edges, approximately 15 to 20 minutes.

4. Serve hot or at room temperature.

Stir-Fried Cabbage with Daikon and Carrots ■ ■ ■ ■

Ingredients:

1 tablespoon coconut oil or ghee

2 carrots, julienned

1 3-inch to 4-inch piece daikon, julienned

5 scallions, chopped

1 to 2 garlic cloves

6 cups finely shredded green cabbage

2 tablespoons filtered water

Celtic sea salt, to taste

¼ teaspoon dried thyme

1 teaspoon fresh lemon juice, or to taste

Directions:

1. Heat coconut oil or ghee in a large skillet or wok over medium-high heat. Add carrots, daikon, scallions and garlic, and cook for 1 minute, stirring constantly. Add cabbage and stir-fry for 2 minutes. Add water, salt and thyme.

2. Cover and cook for 5 to 8 minutes, stirring occasionally, until cabbage is tender. Reduce heat if necessary.

3. Transfer to a serving dish, sprinkle with lemon juice, and serve immediately.

Your family will love the taste of this stir-fried cabbage! It's crisp and sweet, and the lemon adds a tangy finish.

Savory Red Chard with Garlic

■ ■ ■ ■ ■ ■ ■

Ingredients:

1 bunch red chard, stems removed and
    chopped

Filtered water

1 to 2 tablespoons coconut oil or ghee

3 garlic cloves, minced

½ teaspoon cumin

½ teaspoon paprika

1 tablespoon lemon juice

Celtic sea salt, to taste

Directions:

1. Heat coconut oil or ghee in a saucepan.
Add garlic, cumin and paprika and sauté 30
seconds, being careful not to overcook the
spices.

2. Add chard stems and sauté until soft. Add
chard leaves and continue to cook until they
soften, about 3 minutes. (Add a few tablespoons of filtered water if pan is dry.)

3. Season to taste with lemon juice and sea
salt. Serve hot.

Simmered Greens

■ ■ ■ ■ ■ ■ ■

Ingredients:

1 tablespoon coconut oil or ghee

1 red onion, sliced

2 garlic cloves, crushed

1 tablespoon fresh ginger, minced

2 bunches collard greens, stems removed
    and roughly chopped

1 quart homemade vegetable stock
    (page 57)

2 cups filtered water

1 head cabbage, thinly sliced

Directions:

1. In a large stockpot, melt coconut oil or ghee
and sauté onions until soft. Add garlic, ginger,
and greens. Continue to cook for 3 to 5
minutes, or until greens darken in color.

2. Add stock and water. Bring to a boil and
boil for 1 minute. Lower heat to medium and
allow to simmer for 20 minutes, or until about
half of the water evaporates.

3. Add cabbage and cook an additional 20
minutes, or until cabbage is thoroughly
cooked and most of the cooking liquids have
evaporated.

Spinach with Almonds

■ ■ ■ ■ ■ ■ ■

Ingredients:

2 tablespoons olive oil, coconut oil or ghee

2 tablespoons almonds, soaked for at least 8 hours, chopped

½ onion, diced small

1 one-pound bag of fresh spinach

2 teaspoons freshly squeezed lemon juice

Celtic sea salt, to taste

Directions:

1. Sauté chopped almonds in 1 tablespoon of coconut oil or ghee. When lightly browned, remove from pan and set aside.

2. Melt the remaining tablespoon of coconut oil or ghee in large pot. "Sweat" onions over low to medium heat for 3 to 4 minutes. When partially translucent, turn to low heat and add fresh spinach. Cover and cook. Stir occasionally as spinach reduces.

3. Add almonds and lemon juice to the spinach and sprinkle with sea salt. Serve immediately.

Stir-fried Carrots with Lime and Cumin

■ ■ ■ ■ ■ ■ ■

Ingredients:

2 tablespoons coconut oil or ghee

2 teaspoons mustard seeds

½ fresh Serrano chile, minced

3 small dried Thai or other small chiles

1 teaspoon cumin seeds

1 garlic clove, minced

1½ pounds carrots, grated

Juice of 1 lime or ½ lemon

1 bunch fresh chives, chopped

1 teaspoon Celtic sea salt or to taste

Directions:

1. Cook mustard seeds in coconut oil or ghee in a wok until seeds pop, about 1 or 2 minutes. Add chiles, cumin seeds, and garlic. Stir until garlic begins to brown.

2. Add carrots, stirring until warmed through, approximately 5 to 7 minutes. Squeeze lemon or lime over the carrots and sprinkle with chives. Remove from heat and season with sea salt. Remove the dried chiles. Serve hot or cold.

If you prefer a more "smoky" chile taste you can use ¼ of a dried ancho chile in place of the Thai chiles.

Turnips with Spinach and Garlic ■ ■ ■ ■ ■ ■ ■ ■

Ingredients:

3 tablespoons coconut oil or ghee

2 pounds turnips, peeled and diced

6 garlic cloves, minced

1 cup spinach, chopped

1 onion, chopped

¾ cup homemade vegetable stock
    (page 57) or filtered water

Celtic sea salt, to taste

Directions:

1. Sauté turnips in 2 tablespoons of coconut oil or ghee for 3 minutes. Remove from pan with a slotted spoon. Add garlic and spinach. Sauté for 30 seconds or until moisture from spinach evaporates. Remove from pan.

2. Sauté onion in remaining tablespoon of coconut oil or ghee for 5 minutes until onion begins to brown.

3. Add vegetable stock or filtered water, bring to a boil. Add turnips and cover. Lower heat and simmer for 15 minutes.

4. Add spinach, cook for an additional 5 minutes or until turnips are tender. Season to taste with sea salt.

Yellow Squash with Carrots, Syrian Style ■ ■ ■ ■ ■ ■ ■ ■

Ingredients:

1 tablespoon coconut oil or ghee

1 onion, chopped

½ pound carrots

½ pound yellow summer squash

½ pound zucchini

½ cup filtered water

1½ teaspoons dried mint

2 garlic cloves

1 tablespoon Lakanto

2 tablespoons freshly squeezed lemon juice

Celtic sea salt, to taste

Directions:

1. Trim carrots and squash and cut into ½ inch slices.

2. Sauté onion in coconut oil or ghee for 5 minutes, or until golden brown. Add carrots and squash and sauté for 2 minutes.

3. Add water, mint, garlic and Lakanto. Cover and cook over medium heat for 5 minutes, or until vegetables are tender.

4. Remove from heat, add lemon juice, and season with sea salt according to taste. Serve hot.

Curry Cauliflower "Mashed Potatoes" ■ ■ ■ ■ ■ ■ ■

Ingredients:

1 to 2 tablespoons coconut oil or ghee

1 large onion, chopped

2 garlic cloves, minced

1½ teaspoons fresh ginger root, grated

1 tablespoon curry powder, or to taste

¼ teaspoon cayenne pepper

1 head of cauliflower, chopped

¼ cup filtered water

Celtic sea salt, Herbamare, or Trocomare, to taste

Lemon juice, to taste

Directions:

1. Sauté onion, garlic, ginger root, curry powder, and cayenne pepper in coconut oil or ghee to soften and blend flavors. Add cauliflower and filtered water. Simmer or pressure cook until tender.

2. Mash ingredients using a potato masher.

3. Add sea salt, Herbamare or Trocomare and lemon juice, according to taste.

Super Savoy Cabbage and Celery Stir-Fry ■ ■ ■ ■ ■ ■ ■

Ingredients:

1 tablespoon coconut oil or ghee

2 garlic cloves, minced

2 celery stalks, thinly sliced

6 cups savoy cabbage, shredded

Pinch Celtic sea salt

Raw, organic apple cider vinegar or lemon juice, to taste

Directions:

1. Heat coconut oil or ghee in a large skillet or wok over high heat. Add garlic and cook for 5 to10 seconds. Add celery and stir vigorously for 30 seconds. Add cabbage and stir-fry approximately 1 minute.

2. Sprinkle with sea salt, reduce heat to medium-high, cover, and cook for approximately 2 more minutes. Stir a few times to avoid burning.

3. Remove from heat when cabbage is bright green and slightly crunchy. Serve with a splash of apple cider vinegar or lemon juice.

Stir-frying is a healthy way to prepare a meal and lightly cooking these vegetables preserves their essential nutrients.

Sweet and Sour Cabbage

■ ■ □ ■ ■ ■ □

Ingredients:

1 tablespoon coconut oil or ghee

1 large Vidalia or other sweet onion, julienned

1 head of cabbage, cored, julienned

1 head of red cabbage, cored, julienned

½ teaspoon coriander

½ teaspoon cardamom

½ cup raw, organic apple cider vinegar

1 teaspoon Lakanto

Directions:

1. Heat coconut oil or ghee in stockpot over medium heat. Sauté onion until translucent and lightly caramelized. Add both types of cabbage and mix well.

2. Mix Lakanto with apple cider vinegar and dissolve thoroughly. Add the Lakanto and apple cider vinegar mixture to vegetables. Season with the dry spices. Cover and simmer over medium-low heat. Stir frequently until cabbage is soft and fragrant.

This quick and delicious dish can be added to any meal! The sweetness comes from no-calorie zero-glycemic Lakanto. This is great as a side dish with turkey sausages.

Starchy vegetables can provide a hearty, comforting meal that really hits the spot, especially during cold winter months! You can enjoy red-skin new potatoes, water chestnuts, winter squash, artichokes, Jerusalem artichokes, and English peas as entrees, but take care to combine them only with the four B.E.D. grain-like seeds and non-starchy vegetables. Red-skin potatoes are the only potatoes on The Body Ecology Diet (feel free to eat the skins). Sweet corn is only mildly starchy when cooked; when eaten raw, it is a non-starchy vegetable. Lima beans digest best when combined with non-starchy veggies. Remember to never eat too many starchy veggies in one meal, and do limit yourself to one helping of grain. If you're still hungry, eat more alkaline-forming land or ocean vegetables.

Gingery Quinoa and Potato Patties ■ ■ ■ ■ ■ ■ ■

Ingredients:

¾ cup red or sweet potatoes, peeled

1 cup quinoa, soaked for 8 hours, cooked

Filtered water

1 cup kale, chopped fine

½ cup carrot, finely shredded

⅓ cup celery, finely chopped

⅓ cup quick-cooking oats

¼ cup frozen peas, thawed

2 tablespoons red onion, finely chopped

1 tablespoon garlic, minced

2½ teaspoons fresh ginger, peeled, grated

¼ teaspoon fine sea salt

Directions:

1. Cook red or sweet potatoes in boiling water until very soft, about 15 minutes. Drain and set aside to cool.

2. Preheat oven to 400 degrees.

3. Combine all ingredients in a large bowl. Using your hands or a wooden spoon, blend until ingredients hold together. Form into patties about 4 inches in diameter and ¾-inch thick.

4. Arrange on parchment paper and bake for 15 minutes. Turn patties and bake for another 15 minutes until browned.

Curried Indian Potatoes and Cauliflower ■ ■ ■ ■ ■ ■ ■

Ingredients:

2 tablespoons coconut oil or ghee

2 medium onions, diced

8 cups red-skin potatoes, diced

1 head cauliflower, cut into small florets

2 teaspoons Trocomare or Herbamare

1 teaspoon curry powder

1 cup filtered water

¼ cup mint leaves, julienned

Directions:

1. Heat coconut oil or ghee in a large pot. Add onions and cook until translucent. Add potatoes and continue to cook over high heat until almost soft. Add cauliflower, Trocomare, curry powder and filtered water. Reduce heat, cover, and cook until vegetables are tender. Stir in mint leaves. Blend mixture well.

2. Serve hot or at room temperature.

Butternut Squash and Potato Mash ■ ■ ■ ■ ■ ■ ■

Ingredients:

1 butternut squash (approximately
   2 pounds), halved lengthwise, seeded

Filtered water

1 pound red-skin potatoes

1 tablespoon Celtic sea salt

4 tablespoons coconut oil or ghee

1 tablespoon fresh rosemary, chopped

1 teaspoon fresh thyme, chopped

Directions:

1. Preheat oven to 400 degrees.

2. Place squash cut side down in baking pan. Add 1 cup filtered water and bake 40 to 45 minutes until squash is tender when pierced with a fork. Remove from oven, and set aside until cool enough to handle.

3. Steam or boil potatoes and add 1 teaspoon of sea salt. When tender, remove from heat and drain.

4. Scoop out warm squash and combine with potatoes.

5. Heat coconut oil or ghee in small sauté pan. Add rosemary and thyme and stir for approximately 1 minute until herbs release aroma. Add the ghee, herbs, and remaining salt to squash and potatoes.

6. Mash ingredients to desired consistency. Serve warm.

Potato-Stuffed Peppers (Bharwaan Mirchee) ■ ■ ■ ■

Ingredients:

1½ pounds red-skin potatoes, peeled

8 small red bell peppers

1 teaspoon coriander seeds

1 teaspoon cumin seeds

¼ teaspoon cayenne pepper

1 tablespoon fresh mint, chopped

½ hot, fresh green chile, seeded, minced

2 teaspoons fresh cilantro, chopped

1 lemon or 2 limes, juiced

1 teaspoon Celtic sea salt

Directions:

1. Preheat oven to 400 degrees.

2. Cook, drain, and mash potatoes.

3. Cut "caps" off of bell peppers and scoop out seeds. Set aside.

4. Toast coriander and cumin seeds in a dry skillet until fragrant, about 1 to 2 minutes. Grind with a mortar and pestle and add to mashed potatoes.

5. Add remaining ingredients to the potatoes and stir well.

6. Fill peppers with potato mixture and bake for 30 minutes, or until peppers are tender.

With the exception of sushi, most of us have had little experience with eating "seaweed," which is unfortunate because there is so much good packed into even a small amount of ocean veggies! Unlike our depleted soil, the sea is rich in minerals and trace elements. Vegetables harvested from the ocean are a significant source of calcium, magnesium and iron, and they're one of the few vegetable sources of vitamin B12. Also, red and green seaweeds are the best inexpensive source to provide your daily iodine requirements. Rich in soluble fiber, ocean vegetables can help you feel full, aid your digestive processes, and promote the growth of microflora in your gut. You will be very surprised by how tasty these gifts from the sea can be. We encourage you to be adventurous and try these wonderful recipes!

Cucumber, Wakame, and Red Pepper Salad ■ ■ ■ ■ ■

Ingredients:

½ ounce dry wakame

Filtered water

4 large cucumbers, peeled, very thinly sliced

2 teaspoons Herbamare or Celtic sea salt

1 large red bell pepper, diced

1 small red onion, finely diced

⅓ cup raw, organic apple cider vinegar

2 tablespoons organic, unrefined flax seed oil or pumpkin seed oil

Directions:

1. Cover wakame with filtered water and soak for 15 minutes.

2. Sprinkle Herbamare or sea salt on cucumbers and allow to rest for several minutes to release their liquid. Drain.

3. Drain wakame and discard the soaking water. Remove and discard wakame "stem," chop, and add to cucumbers. Add diced red bell pepper and red onion.

4. Toss salad with apple cider vinegar and oil.

Hijiki with Onions and Carrots ■ ■ ■ ■ ■ ■ ■

Ingredients:

2 ounces dry hijiki

Filtered water

1 large onion, diced

2 large carrots, diced

1 teaspoon coconut oil

Celtic sea salt, to taste

Directions:

1. Cover hijiki in filtered water and soak for 15 minutes. Drain and discard soaking water. Chop.

2. Sauté onion in coconut oil. Add carrots and hijiki. Cover with water and simmer for 45 minutes to 1 hour, checking occasionally to make sure water has not evaporated.

3. Add sea salt to taste during the last 10 minutes of cooking.

Arame is a nice substitute for the hijiki in this recipe! You can also stir in some just-cooked, diced red-skin potatoes and/or steamed peas right before serving.

To create one of our most popular salads, we chill this basic recipe, toss with leafy lettuce and top with The Body Ecology Diet Salad Dressing (page 94).

Agar-Jelled Butternut Squash

■ ■ ■ ■ ■ ■ ■

Ingredients:

3 cups filtered water

5 to 6 tablespoon agar flakes

1 small onion, diced

4 cups butternut squash, diced

1 teaspoon Celtic sea salt or Herbamare

½ teaspoon dried dill

You can substitute carrots, broccoli, or cauliflower in place of squash. Top with your favorite salad dressing!

For a spicier version, add 1 teaspoon Spice Hunter curry seasoning.

For a sweeter version, use 1 teaspoon Frontier Herbs butterscotch alcohol-free extract and Body Ecology's stevia liquid concentrate, to taste.

Directions:

1. Place filtered water and agar flakes in a pot. Bring to a boil, stirring frequently to dissolve the flakes. Add squash, onion, and sea salt or Herbamare. Reduce heat to medium-low and simmer until tender.

2. Purée in a blender until smooth. Add dill.

3. Pour hot purée into oiled gelatin mold. Refrigerate until set.

4. Slice and serve garnished with parsley, thinly sliced red bell pepper strips, and a dollop of Classic Homemade Mayonnaise (page 94). (A pinch of curry and/or ginger can be added to the mayonnaise.) A good vinaigrette also makes a nice topping. Sprinkle slivers of toasted, sprouted almonds on top.

Sea Palm and Zucchini Salad

Ingredients:

3 ounces dried sea palm

2 scallions, greens only, chopped

1 zucchini, diced

½ carrot, minced

½ daikon radish, finely diced

¼ red, yellow or orange bell pepper, minced

2 tablespoons fresh ginger, grated

1 garlic clove, minced

1 teaspoon Celtic sea salt

3 tablespoons Dijon mustard

3 tablespoons pumpkinseed oil

Directions:

1. Soak sea palm until soft. Rinse and chop into large pieces.

2. Toss the sea palm with remaining ingredients in a large bowl and allow the salad to marinate for 2 to 3 hours before serving.

Notes

Notes

Notes

Grain-Like Seeds ■ ■ ■ ■

A whole new world of exciting flavors will open up for you and your family when you explore recipes for the four Body Ecology grain-like seeds: millet, quinoa, buckwheat, and amaranth. You may be used to eating a lot of wheat and rice, as well as breads and cereals, but if you try our recipes with an open mind your cravings for these "common" breads and grains will diminish and then totally disappear.

Try to eat a meal with these grain-like seeds (with vegetables, of course!) at least once a day. When soaked and then cooked with herbs, vegetables, and seasonings, these healing grains become even more flavorful.

As a rule, soaking these grains in water for 8 hours before cooking is a must to remove the phytic acid. Doing so makes them easier to digest. Be sure to wash them well: quinoa has a bitter outer coating, and millet tends to carry a lot of "dirt." Use a very fine mesh strainer (particularly for amaranth and quinoa), and rinse these seeds under running water for a couple of minutes before cooking.

The basic water-to-grain/seed ratio is 2 to 1 for quinoa and buckwheat, although it can vary according to taste, recipe, and method of cooking (e.g., pressure cooker). A 3 to 1 ratio of water-to-grain/seed is better for amaranth and millet.

You will add sea salt to most of these grain dishes, but salt is particularly important when cooking buckwheat. Buckwheat is acid forming and needs salt in the cooking water to make it more alkaline. Of course we recommend Celtic sea salt from Selina Naturally™!

Roasting Millet or Quinoa

Pour soaked and rinsed seeds into a dry skillet over very low heat and stir slowly until the grain dries and you smell a nutty aroma. (Millet will not brown.)

Roasting millet and quinoa before cooking brings out a particularly good, nutty taste.

In addition to the recipes in this section, here are some suggestions for simple ways to use The Body Ecology Diet grain-like seeds:

Make cream of buckwheat or quinoa flakes sweet with stevia, cinnamon, vanilla, and ghee. Or for a more savory flavor, toss in some small squares of nori as the grains cook. Make amaranth with dulse then add ghee and a pinch of cayenne pepper. Serve quinoa or amaranth sautéed in olive oil with carrots, peas, and onions. All of the grain-like seeds are very compatible with red potatoes. Mash potatoes and buckwheat with herbs and make patties or croquettes to sauté in coconut oil. Buckwheat also goes well with corn, cabbage, onions, and many of the organic herbal seasoning blends.

For summertime lunches, toss pre-cooked millet or quinoa into a fresh green salad or with a cooked vegetable dish served at room temperature.

You can make any number of sauces from puréed Body Ecology soups, such as Creamy Dilled Cauliflower (page 56), or try Annmarie's Gingery Carrot Sauce (page 109). Spoon them over any of the grain-like seeds and enjoy!

Oxalates in Grain-like Seeds

Oxalates are a plant poison that is naturally found in the roots, leaves and stems of some of the most nutritious vegetables. Think of oxalates as thousands of tiny shards of glass with pointy edges that discourage insects from eating the plant. Generally oxalates are not harmful to humans because our intestinal microbiota eat them and they leave the body in our stools. But if antibiotics have destroyed the microbiota and/or if you have a leaky gut from a high-sugar, high-fat diet and chronic stress, these glass-like shards can cause problems. Until your gut lining is healed and you have reestablished a healthy inner ecosystem on The Body Ecology Diet you'll want to be on a medium to low-oxalate diet.

When you have a systemic candida infection, your oxalate consumption should be minimized. Some people will need to avoid them entirely. While the connection between oxalates and yeast infections is not yet fully understood, having candidaisis makes you more sensitive to oxalates and eating them can make your symptoms more acute. The Body Ecology Diet is a sugar-free, gluten-free probiotic diet that will help you conquer the candidiasis. Until you do your motto is: Don't count calories, count oxalates.

Foods high in oxalates include chocolate, spinach, unfermented soy foods, sweet potatoes, nuts and seeds. Ideally they should be completely avoided. These foods are also very high in copper. If you suffer from Hashimoto's or hypothyroidism, they can disrupt the balance between zinc and copper causing a zinc deficiency and symptoms of fatigue and hypothyroidism. For more information, we suggest reading *Why Am I Always So Tired?* by Anne Louise Gittleman.

Because they are seeds, quinoa, millet, amaranth and buckwheat are also high in oxalates, which is why we have included this information on oxalates in this section. In the beginning you may want to skip these grain-like seeds altogether. See how you feel when you eat them. However, avoiding the oxalates in the four nourishing grain-like seeds is simple: first soak them, then boil them. The recipe "Heavenly Quinoa Hash" on page 148 has an example of how to do this.

Oxalates are best known for causing kidney stones, but other common symptoms include extreme fatigue, fibromyalgia, and pain (especially in the eye, muscles and joints, and when urinating). Sandy stools are another sign of oxalate damage. People with COPD, asthma, cystic fibrosis, Hashimoto's disease, hypothyroidism, vulvodynia or genital pain should be on a low-oxalate diet.

Why Not Skip the Grain-like Seeds?

You certainly can, but you will find that grains and grain-like seeds, properly prepared, add fiber to your diet and help feed friendly bacteria. The fiber helps hold water to soften your stool and provides bulk that helps with elimination. A robust, diverse gut microbiome is very important in order to metabolize carbohydrates. The bacteria chew them up and spit them out as important fatty acids including butyric acid, which helps keep your gut lining healthy. The thyroid, adrenals, brain and intestines are healthier when you eat small amounts of complex carbs and grain-like seeds. Be sure to eat them with fermented foods and drinks. The bacteria will not only help digest them, they will also eat the sugars in these fiber-rich foods.

Eventually you can add real grains to your meals such as whole oats, barley and various rices. (GABA rice and red rice are tasty varieties.) Remember to soak them and cook slowly as if you were making porridge and combine with lots of vegetables to ensure that your meal is more alkaline.

Oxalobacter formigenes is the primary eater of oxalates and becomes a resident in the inner ecosystem of babies when they begin crawling. *O. formigenes* is easily destroyed by antibiotics and rarely recolonizes. It is an oxygen-loving bacterium and is not found in fermented foods and is not available as a supplement. Fortunately a few other bacteria have the genes to consume oxalates, including *Bifidus lactis*, *Bifidus infantis* and *Lactobacillus plantarum*. Cultured vegetables made with the BE starter have an abundance of *L. plantarum* so when you eat plant foods have a serving of fermented veggies too.

The Bottom Line: Avoid high oxalate foods until your leaky gut has healed, your yeast infection is under control, and you have established a healthy inner ecosystem by eating fermented foods rich in the oxalate-eating bacteria *L. plantarum*. Take probiotic supplements, especially *Bifidus infantis* and *Bifidus lactis*. Lastly, enjoy the recipes here! If you believe you are sensitive to oxalates become an "oxalate accountant" and count the total amount of oxalates you consume in a day—ideally under 40 to 60 milligrams). For more information on oxalates and a chart about high, medium, and low oxalate foods, join the Yahoo group called Trying Low Oxalates owned by Susan Owens.

Cooking Grain-Like Seeds to Reduce Oxalates

To eliminate the oxalates in grain-like seeds simply boil them in a pot of hot water like you would pasta.

INSTRUCTIONS:

1. Soak seeds 8 hours or overnight in water, pour off soaking water, rinse and drain.
2. Bring a large pot of water to a rolling boil and add sea salt.
3. Add soaked grain-like seeds to boiling water.
4. Cook for appropriate amount of time (see cooking times below) then drain into a colander that has very small holes. Rinse under hot water if desired. They are now ready to eat.
5. Quinoa and millet can also be placed in a hot cast iron skillet at this point and roasted if desired.

Other ways to use the pot-boiled seeds:

- Chill, add vegetables and a salad dressing and make them into a grain/seed salad.
- Shape them into croquettes and sauté in ghee or coconut oil then serve with a gravy or sauce.

Boiling times to reduce oxalates:

- Quinoa cooks in 11 minutes.
- Millet, buckwheat and amaranth cook in 15 minutes.

Autism and Oxalates

Children with autism are often very sensitive to oxalates, but some parents have found that suddenly eliminating all oxalates from an autistic child's diet often makes the initial oxalate symptoms return. This is caused by the body's attempt to eliminate them all at once ("dumping"). To avoid this, reduce the amounts of dietary oxalates each day, slowly eliminating them entirely over a year's time. However, at Body Ecology we have found that if enemas and colonics are done when the symptoms of oxalate dumping are noted, this prolonged withdrawal should not be necessary. Children on the autistic spectrum struggle with methylation problems and cannot clear toxins easily. The body can eliminate some oxalates through the lungs and skin, and having a healthy liver that can clear these toxins is important, but ultimately toxins must be eliminated in the stool, which is why we encourage the use of home enemas and colon hydrotherapy.

Basic Amaranth—Pressure Cooked

Ingredients:

1 cup amaranth, soaked for at least 8 hours

2 cups filtered water

¼ teaspoon Celtic sea salt, or to taste

1 tablespoon coconut oil or ghee (optional)

To cook amaranth without using a pressure cooker, simply add the soaked seeds to 2 cups of boiling water and cook for 15 minutes.

Directions:

1. Combine the amaranth, water, and sea salt in pressure cooker. Adjust heat to maintain high pressure and cook for 6 minutes.

2. Reduce pressure with a quick-release method. Remove the lid, tilting it away from you to allow any excess steam to escape.

3. Stir well, adding coconut oil or ghee, if desired. If the mixture is too thin, simmer while stirring constantly until thickened, about 30 seconds.

Basic Buckwheat

Ingredients:

1 cup buckwheat, soaked for at least 8 hours

2 cups filtered water

1 teaspoon Celtic sea salt, or to taste

Directions:

1. Rinse soaked buckwheat in a strainer.

2. Bring water and salt to a boil in a saucepan.

3. Add buckwheat, cover, and reduce heat. Simmer until all the water is absorbed, approximately 15 minutes.

For a rich, nutty flavor, toast buckwheat (with or without organic, unrefined coconut oil or ghee) in a skillet, stirring constantly, before adding to the water.

Basic Millet

Ingredients:

1 cup millet, soaked for at least 8 hours

3 cups filtered water

1 teaspoon Celtic sea salt, or to taste

Directions:

1. Rinse soaked millet in a strainer.

2. Bring water and salt to a boil.

3. Add millet, cover, and reduce heat. Simmer for 25 to 30 minutes.

4. To increase fluffiness, remove from heat and let stand covered for 5 to 10 minutes.

For an even more delicious flavor, roast millet in a heavy skillet until millet has a nutty aroma. For fluffy millet, boil water and salt before adding millet. If you start grains or grain-like seeds in cold water, they become creamier and sticky.

Basic Quinoa

Ingredients:

1 cup quinoa, soaked for at least 8 hours

2 cups filtered water

1 pinch Celtic sea salt

For a rich, nutty flavor, toast quinoa in a skillet, stirring constantly, before adding to the water.

Directions:

1. Rinse soaked quinoa in a strainer.

2. Bring water and salt to a rapid boil in a saucepan.

3. Add quinoa, cover, and reduce heat. Simmer until all the water is absorbed and the grains become translucent and pop open, approximately 15 to 25 minutes.

Bill and Mike's Waffles

Ingredients:

2 cups flour (amaranth, half amaranth and half millet, or another grain flour combination)

½ teaspoon Celtic sea salt

¼ cup ghee or coconut oil

2 teaspoons baking powder, aluminum-free

2 eggs, whites and yolks separated

1 to 1 ⅓ cups filtered water

Directions:

1. Preheat waffle iron to medium or dark setting. A little experimentation will determine which setting is best.

2. Whisk flour, sea salt, and baking powder in mixing bowl.

3. In separate bowl, whisk egg yolks, water, and melted coconut oil or ghee until barely blended.

4. Add egg-yolk mixture to the flour mixture and whisk until a smooth, pourable batter forms. Add water if batter is too thick.

5. In separate bowl, beat egg whites until they form soft peaks. Fold egg whites into batter by hand; do not overmix.

6. Using a glass or plastic measuring cup (aluminum causes batter to break down), pour about 1 cup of batter evenly into all areas of waffle iron.

6. Waffles should cook in 10 to 14 minutes. Check the waffles when steam stops rising from waffle iron. They should be crisp and brown. Cool extra waffles on wire rack.

Waffles, like any flour-based food, should be an occasional meal. They go nicely with vegetable soup at any time of day. We even use them to make sandwiches with Classic Homemade Mayonnaise (page 94) and a variety of roasted or grilled veggies! The waffles freeze well or they can be kept for several days in the refrigerator.

Heidi's Onion Pie

Ingredients:

2 cups amaranth flour

1 teaspoon Celtic sea salt

4 tablespoons coconut oil or ghee

½ cup filtered water

6 large onions, thinly sliced in ½ rounds

4 garlic cloves, minced

1 tablespoon Italian blend *or* oregano,
parsley, rosemary, basil, and celery seed

½ teaspoon basil

Pinch of red pepper flakes

1 tablespoon coconut oil or ghee

1 cup filtered water

1½ to 2 teaspoons Celtic sea salt

½ cup amaranth, soaked for at least 8
hours and rinsed

½ red bell pepper, minced

2 to 3 scallions, thinly sliced in rounds

1 tablespoon fresh herbs such as basil *or*
cilantro, minced (optional)

Herbamare, garlic powder, red pepper
flakes, to taste

Directions:

1. Preheat oven to 400 degrees.

2. Make the crust in a bowl or in a food processor. Combine amaranth flour, sea salt, and coconut oil or ghee and cut or pulse until crumbly. Gradually add water until dough begins to form a ball.

3. Turn dough out onto waxed paper and form into flat round. Sprinkle flour over and around the dough, top with more waxed paper, and roll until ¼ inch thick.

4. Transfer the crust to a round pizza pan. Crimp edges. Pierce the dough all over with a fork to keep it from shrinking. Bake for 10 minutes, remove from oven, and set aside.

5. Sauté onion, garlic, herbs, and pepper flakes in coconut oil or ghee. Reduce heat, cover, and cook until onions are tender, approximately 15 minutes.

6. Add water, sea salt, and amaranth. Bring to a boil, cover, and reduce heat. Simmer covered, for approximately 20 minutes. Remove lid and boil off excess liquid. (You can also prepare the amaranth in a pressure cooker (see the first recipe in this section). Rinse and drain before proceeding.

7. Combine red bell pepper, scallions, and optional fresh herbs and add to hot amaranth.

8. Spoon the filling evenly over pre-baked crust. Sprinkle with Herbamare, garlic powder, and pepper flakes, if desired.

9. Bake pie for approximately 20 minutes or until lightly browned.

Heidi's South of the Border Savory Crackers ■ ■ ■ ■ ■ ■ ■

Ingredients:

½ cup amaranth flour

½ cup blue corn flour

¼ cup arrowroot powder

¼ teaspoon Celtic sea salt

½ teaspoon baking soda

½ teaspoon chili powder

½ teaspoon cumin seed

3 tablespoons coconut oil or ghee

5 tablespoons filtered water

Herbamare, to taste

Directions:

1. Heat oven to 350 degrees.

2. Sift or thoroughly blend dry ingredients and spices. Using a whisk, pastry cutter, or fork, work coconut oil or ghee into flour mixture. Stir in just enough water to make dough form a ball.

3. On a floured surface, or between waxed paper, roll dough flat (approximately ¼ inch thick). Sprinkle dough lightly with Herbamare. Cut into fun shapes using a cookie cutter.

4. Transfer crackers to an oiled cookie sheet.

5. Bake for 15 minutes or until edges just begin to brown. Cool on a wire rack. Before serving, place rack of crackers on cookie sheet and return to oven for a few minutes to become crisp.

Steamed Amaranth Pudding ■ ■ ■ ■ ■ ■ ■

Ingredients:

1 cup amaranth, soaked for at least 8 hours

1 bunch scallions, chopped

2 teaspoons chives

2 teaspoons fresh cilantro

2 teaspoons fresh basil

2 teaspoons fresh parsley

2 teaspoons fresh dill

3 to 4 cups vegetable stock (page 57)

2 tablespoons coconut oil or ghee

Celtic sea salt, to taste

Directions:

1. Preheat oven to 350 degrees.

2. Cook soaked amaranth in the vegetable stock until it becomes sticky. Stir remaining ingredients into the hot amaranth and season to taste.

3. Scoop amaranth into individual baking dishes and bake in a water bath for 25 minutes, or until puddings are firm and tops are golden.

Vegetarian Kasha "Meatloaf"

■ ■ ■ ■ ■ ■ ■

Ingredients:

2 tablespoons coconut oil or ghee

1 medium onion, chopped

4 garlic cloves, chopped

4 stalks of celery, chopped

1 red bell pepper, seeded, diced (optional)

1 tablespoon chili powder blend, or to taste

Celtic sea salt, to taste

2 ears fresh corn, cut off the cob

2 cups fresh spinach, cabbage, or kale,
  chopped

1 can water chestnuts, drained, chopped
  (optional)

1 cup buckwheat, cooked

1 bunch scallions, sliced

Directions:

1. Preheat oven to 400 degrees.

2. Heat coconut oil or ghee in a large skillet. Sauté onion, garlic, celery, and bell pepper until soft. Add chili powder blend, sea salt, corn, greens, and water chestnuts. Sauté until soft.

3. Add cooked buckwheat to the skillet and sauté until blended. Adjust seasonings then fold in scallions. Pour mixture into an oiled loaf pan or casserole dish. Bake at 400 degrees for 45 to 60 minutes.

4. Serve slices with a sauce such as Annmarie's Gingery Carrot Sauce (page 109) or the Body Ecology Gluten-Free Gravy (page 111).

For a flavorful variation, scoop the seeds and membranes from 4 red bell peppers or carve out the centers of 4 onions, then stuff with loaf mixture and bake at 350 degrees for 30 minutes. You can also roll it in steamed cabbage leaves and bake them the same way.

Buckwheat Veggie Stew

■ ■ ■ ■ ■ ■ ■

Ingredients:

2 tablespoons coconut oil or ghee

2 cups corn kernels, fresh or frozen

3 cups savoy cabbage, chopped

1 large onion, chopped

½ red bell pepper, minced

4 cups vegetable stock (page 57) or water

1¼ teaspoons Celtic sea salt

1 tablespoon organic meatloaf seasoning,
  or similar, to taste

2 cups roasted buckwheat, soaked for
  8 hours

¼ to ½ cup parsley, minced

Directions:

1. Sauté all the vegetables except parsley in coconut oil or ghee for about 5 minutes. Add vegetable stock or water, salt, and seasoning. Bring to a boil.

2. Add buckwheat and simmer for 20 minutes.

3. Remove from heat, fold in parsley, and allow to stand, covered, for 10 minutes.

This recipe is a hearty vegetarian meal, great for cold weather!

We like the extensive selection of organic herbs, spices, and blends made by Spicely Organics (spicely.com). Their meatloaf blend is excellent in this stew!

Buckwheat "Burgers"

■ ■ ◻ ■ ■ ■ ◻

Ingredients:

3 tablespoons coconut oil or ghee

1 large onion, minced

2 stalks celery, finely minced

2 garlic cloves, finely minced

½ cup parsley, finely minced

1 carrot, finely grated

3 cups homemade vegetable broth
   (page 57) or water

2 cups cracked, roasted buckwheat,
   soaked for 8 hours

1 teaspoon Herbamare

½ teaspoon Celtic sea salt

1 tablespoon curry seasoning, or your
   favorite herbal blend

½ cup arrowroot powder

1 cup millet, quinoa, or amaranth flour

Directions:

1. Sauté onion in 1 tablespoon of coconut oil or ghee until slightly browned. Add celery, garlic, parsley, carrot, and broth or water. Cover and cook for 5 minutes.

2. Add buckwheat, Herbamare, sea salt, curry seasoning, and arrowroot. Cover and cook on low for 10 minutes. Remove from heat and allow to steam, covered, for 10 more minutes.

3. Add your choice of flour, mix well, and set aside. When cool enough to handle, form into patties.

4. Sauté burgers in just enough coconut oil or ghee to prevent sticking. Drain on paper towels and serve.

This is a hardy, home-style meal when served with garlic green beans, a grated carrot salad and cultured vegetables.

Holiday Millet and Amaranth with Herbs

■ ■ ◻ ■ ■ ■ ◻

Ingredients:

1½ cups millet, soaked for at least 8 hours

½ cup amaranth, soaked for at least 8
   hours

6 cups water

2 bay leaves

1 medium onion, diced

2/3 cup celery, diced

3 garlic cloves, minced

1 tablespoon of coconut oil or ghee

2 teaspoons dry sage leaf, crumbled

1 teaspoon dry thyme leaf

1 teaspoon herbs de Provence

Celtic sea salt or Herbamare, to taste

Directions:

1. Bring millet, amaranth, water, and bay leaves to a boil. Cover, reduce heat, and cook for 30 for minutes. Remove bay leaves.

2. Sauté onion, celery and garlic in coconut oil or ghee over medium heat until tender, but still firm. Add herbs and sauté for about 30 seconds to release flavors. Add veggies to cooked grains and stir to combine thoroughly. Add sea salt or Herbamare, to taste.

For a pretty holiday presentation, use a cup or bowl to create a mold. Rinse the cup in cool water, pack with grain mixture, and immediately invert onto a serving plate.

Herbs de Provence is a wonderful herb mixture that, in addition to rosemary, tarragon and thyme, also contains lavender flower. You'll love it!

Millet and Sweet Vegetables

■ ■ ■ ■ ■ ■ ■

Ingredients:

2 cups millet, soaked for 8 hours, rinsed, dry roasted in skillet

2 medium onions, finely chopped

3 carrots, diced

1 small butternut squash, peeled, cubed

1 teaspoon sea salt

5½ cups filtered water

1 tablespoon coconut oil or ghee

Several pinches of herbs such as thyme, rosemary, sage, and celery seed (optional)

Directions:

1. Combine millet and vegetables in a pressure cooker. (This dish can also be prepared in a saucepan. Increase water to 6 cups, add salt, cook over low heat for 30 minutes. Continue to step 3.)

2. Dissolve sea salt in the filtered water and gently pour water around sides of millet and vegetables. Close cover, bring up to pressure, and cook over low heat for 30 minutes. Reduce pressure and open lid.

3. Fold in coconut oil or ghee and herbs. Stir well and serve.

With its sweet vegetables (onions, carrots, and butternut squash), this dish strengthens the spleen/pancreas and stomach. For the first two to three months on The Body Ecology Diet, you may find that butternut squash is too sweet and feeds candida. If so, leave the butternut squash out of this recipe. The onions and carrots will not cause any problems. Better yet, if you eat cultured veggies with this meal, the microflora will eat up the sugar in the squash!

For a creamier consistency, purée the millet and vegetable mixture with coconut oil or ghee in a blender. You can also add one 3-inch strip of kombu to the pressure cooker with the millet and vegetables. The dish will not be as sweet, but it will have extra minerals.

Millet "Mashed Potatoes"

■ ■ ■ ■ ■ ■ ■

Ingredients:

1 tablespoon coconut oil or ghee

1 small onion, chopped

1 cup millet, soaked for at least 8 hours

1 head cauliflower, chopped

3¼ cups filtered water

¼ teaspoon Celtic sea salt

Grass fed butter (optional)

Directions:

1. Sauté onion in coconut oil or ghee in pressure cooker. Add millet and lightly sauté. Stir in cauliflower, water and salt.

2. Bring to pressure, reduce heat, and cook for 25 minutes and all water is absorbed.

3. Mash with potato masher, adding butter if desired.

For a bit more color and a slight change in flavor, add 1 medium chopped carrot when sautéing cauliflower.

Roasted Millet

Ingredients:

2 tablespoons coconut oil or ghee

1½ cups millet, soaked for at least 8 hours, rinsed

4 to 5 cups homemade vegetable stock (page 57)

¼ cup onion, minced

¼ cup carrot, minced

1 garlic clove, peeled, minced

1 stalk celery, minced

Directions:

1. Brown onions in coconut or ghee over medium heat in a deep sauté pan until translucent. Add carrot and garlic and sauté, stirring, for 2 to 3 more minutes.

2. While onions and veggies cook, heat stock just to boiling and set aside.

3. Toast soaked, rinsed millet in a dry skillet for 3 to 5 minutes or until a nutty aroma develops. Add millet to the sautéed vegetables. Carefully pour hot vegetable stock into pan and reduce heat to lowest setting, Cover and simmer 15 to 20 minutes, or until water is absorbed and grain is tender.

Ginger Fried Quinoa

Ingredients:

½ cup coconut oil or ghee, divided

2 tablespoons garlic, minced

2 tablespoons ginger, minced

2 cups leeks, diced

4 cups day-old quinoa

1 teaspoon unrefined sesame oil, divided

1 tablespoon wheat-free tamari, divided

Directions:

1. Heat ¼ cup of coconut oil or ghee in a large skillet. Sauté the garlic and ginger until golden. Remove and drain on a paper towel.

2. Add the leeks to the skillet and sauté until soft but not browned. Add the remaining coconut oil or ghee and sauté quinoa.

3. Create 4 individual servings by packing a quarter of the quinoa in a small bowl (rinse with water first), then invert each onto a plate. Drizzle each plate with equal amounts of sesame oil and tamari and sprinkle with the garlic and ginger.

For a fancier presentation, cook 4 eggs sunny side up in a tablespoon of coconut oil or ghee. Place an egg on top of each quinoa mold and sprinkle the crispy garlic and ginger on the egg whites.

Tex-Mex Millet and Amaranth Corn Casserole ▪ ▪ ▫ ▪ ▫ ▪ ▪ ▫

Ingredients:

1 tablespoon coconut oil or ghee

1½ cups millet, soaked for at least 8 hours
    and rinsed

½ cup amaranth, soaked for at least 8 hours
    and rinsed

1 tablespoon Celtic sea salt

6 cups filtered water

8 ears of fresh corn, kernels removed, or
    16 oz. frozen corn

1 large onion, minced

1 large red bell pepper, seeded, diced

1 mild green chile, diced (optional)

1 teaspoon Herbamare

1¾ teaspoon Frontier Herbs Mexican
    Seasoning, or similar

Directions:

1. Preheat oven to 350 degrees. Butter a 3-quart casserole dish.

2. Sauté onion, green chile, Mexican seasoning, and sea salt in coconut oil or ghee in a stockpot until onion is translucent.

3. Add millet, amaranth, corn, and water and bring to a boil. Cover, lower heat, and simmer for 30 minutes.

4. Fold in bell pepper and Herbamare and adjust seasonings to taste.

5. Pour mixture into prepared casserole dish. Dot with small amounts of ghee, if desired. Bake 30 minutes at 350 degrees.

To bring out more delicious corn flavor, replace the 6 cups of water in the recipe with corn stock. Cut the fresh corn off the cob and simmer the cut corn and the corn cobs in 7 cups of water for 20 minutes. Discard the cobs, purée the stock, and it's ready to use.

If you'd like an Italian-flavored dish instead, you can use 1 tablespoon of Frontier Herbs Italian Seasoning instead of the Mexican Blend. Exchange the corn and green chile for zucchini and shiitake mushrooms.

Curried Quinoa ▪ ▪ ▫ ▪ ▪ ▪ ▫

Ingredients:

2 tablespoons coconut oil or ghee

2 medium onions, diced

1 tablespoon curry powder

1 teaspoon Celtic sea salt or Herbamare

2 cups vegetables, cooked (such as peas,
    corn, red-skin potatoes, red bell pepper,
    cabbage, yellow squash)

2 cups quinoa, soaked for 8 hours and
    cooked

Directions:

1. Heat coconut oil or ghee in a skillet. Add onions, curry powder and sea salt or Herbamare. Sauté for several minutes until onions are translucent.

2. Add your choice of cooked vegetables. Sauté for several minutes, or until heated through. Stir in cooked quinoa and adjust seasonings.

Heavenly Quinoa Hash

■ ■ ▪ ▪ ■ ■ ▪

Ingredients:

1 cup quinoa, soaked for at least 8 hours
   and rinsed

Water to fill tall stockpot

2 teaspoon sea salt

2 tablespoon coconut oil, unsalted butter,
   or ghee

1 large onion, diced

6 garlic cloves, minced

1 teaspoon chopped fresh thyme

1 red bell pepper, diced

2 medium red-skin potatoes

1 teaspoon paprika

¼ cup minced parsley

Herbamare or Celtic sea salt, to taste

Directions:

1. Bring water and sea salt to a rapid boil in a stockpot. Add quinoa. Boil for 12 minutes then drain in a fine-mesh colander.

2. Place whole potatoes in a large pot of water, cover and bring to a boil. Lower heat and simmer until half-cooked, about 15 minutes. Drain. When potatoes are cool enough to handle, peel and cut into ½-inch cubes.

3. Sauté onion in coconut oil, unsalted butter, or ghee in a separate pan until translucent. Add garlic, thyme, and bell pepper and sauté until tender. Add potatoes, paprika, and parsley and sauté for a few minutes more.

4. Fold in cooked quinoa, and sauté until heated. Taste and adjust seasonings. Add Herbamare before serving.

Quinoa Pilaf

■ ■ ▪ ■ ■ ■ ▪

Ingredients:

3 tablespoons coconut oil, unsalted butter
   or ghee

3 small shallots, finely minced

1¼ teaspoons sea salt, divided

4 cups homemade vegetable stock
   (page 57)

1 cup quinoa, soaked for 8 hours, rinsed

1 pinch saffron, steeped in ¼ cup hot
   (not boiling) water

½ carrot, finely minced

½ frozen organic peas

1 bunch parsley, chopped

Directions:

1. Sauté shallots in oil, butter or ghee until slightly translucent.

2. While shallots cook, heat broth to the boiling point and set aside.

3. Add minced carrot and sea salt to shallots and cook for 3 minutes. Stir in quinoa, saffron, and saffron soaking water. Slowly add hot stock to pan. Cover, turn heat to lowest setting and cook for 20 minutes, or until liquid is absorbed.

4. Remove from heat, add peas and stir in parsley. Allow the steam to cook peas and parsley for a few seconds before serving.

Quinoa Summer Salad

Ingredients:

1 tablespoon coconut oil

1 small onion, minced

3 small red-skin potatoes, finely diced

4 cups quinoa, cooked, cooled

3 scallions, sliced

1 garlic clove

1 small cucumber, peeled, cut into half
    moons

1 stalk celery, minced

2 tablespoons parsley

2 to 3 tablespoons pumpkinseed oil

1 to 2 tablespoons Celtic sea salt

1 teaspoon cayenne pepper or hot paprika

Directions:

1. Heat coconut oil in a sauté pan. Sauté the onion and red-skin potatoes until tender. Cool to room temperature.

2. In a large mixing bowl, combine cooked quinoa, scallions, garlic, cucumber and celery. Add the cooled potato and onion mixture and the parsley to the bowl. Stir until all ingredients are evenly distributed.

3. Pour pumpkinseed oil over salad and season with sea salt and cayenne pepper, to taste.

4. Cover and refrigerate for 2 to 4 hours or overnight. Serve chilled or at room temperature.

This dish is great for using leftover quinoa. If you have a busy schedule, it is excellent to have in the fridge for quick, healthy meals on the run. This dish travels well and it is perfect to bring to a picnic or barbecue.

Stuffed Red Peppers

Ingredients:

2 cups cooked quinoa, amaranth, millet, or
    buckwheat

2 tablespoons coconut oil or ghee

1 medium onion, chopped fine

1 teaspoon Celtic sea salt, or to taste

2 tablespoons dried sweet basil

2 tablespoons paprika

6 garlic cloves, minced

2 stalks celery, chopped fine

1 pound greens, such as kale, parboiled 5
    minutes, chopped

6 red bell peppers, seeded, parboiled 5
    minutes

Directions:

1. Preheat oven to 350 degrees.

2. Sauté onion, sea salt, basil and paprika in coconut oil or ghee until onions are translucent. Add the garlic, celery, and greens, and cook until tender.

3. Combine the onion and greens with the cooked grains. Taste, and adjust seasonings.

4. Stuff red peppers with grain mixture and bake in an oiled casserole dish for 45 minutes.

Royal Red Inca Quinoa

Ingredients:

2 tablespoons coconut oil or ghee

2 scallions, sliced

1 shallot, minced

½ stalk celery, chopped

4 cups cooked red quinoa

1 teaspoon garlic powder

3 ounces vegetable stock (page 57)

1 teaspoon Celtic sea salt

2 tablespoons pumpkinseed oil

Directions:

1. Heat coconut oil or ghee in a large sauté pan over medium-high heat. Add scallions, shallots and celery. Sauté for 2 to 3 minutes or until the vegetables begin to soften.

2. Add cooked red quinoa and garlic powder to pan. Cook for an additional 5 minutes. Add the vegetable stock and sea salt and stir well.

3. Drizzle with the pumpkinseed oil and serve immediately.

Notes

Notes

Notes

Meat, Poultry, and Seafood

The best sources of animal proteins on The Body Ecology Diet include fertile eggs, poultry, beef, lamb, and fish. Pork is not recommended. When you go shopping, always choose the highest quality possible.

Many people do not produce the necessary enzymes to properly break down and metabolize their animal protein meals. If that's you, be sure to always use digestive enzymes with hydrochloric acid (HCl) and pepsin, and pancreatic enzymes that work in the small intestine. (Assist for Protein and Dairy™ and Assist SI™ are two enzyme blends made by Body Ecology.)

Cooking protein properly is extremely important to ensure that you digest it and obtain the full nutritional value from eating it. We've been told that protein must be cooked through completely until it's well done to kill any germs or parasites, but doing so makes it rubbery and difficult to digest. This concern started when the USDA realized that commercially raised animals are often sick and contaminated with toxins from their feed and from medications. But animals raised in stress-free, healthy environments are usually free from illness and parasites so that bacteria should not be a concern if the food is refrigerated and stored properly.

Eating fermented vegetables with your meals and drinking probiotic beverages like Inner-gyBiotic™ and CocoBiotic™ not only ensure better digestion of your protein meals, their beneficial bacteria and yeast will help protect against pathogenic bacteria and parasites that might be present. We highly recommend that you always include something fermented with every protein meal, even eggs.

On The Body Ecology Diet, we also recommend cooking low and slow. When cooking a steak, a burger or a lamb chop, medium rare is preferable. Roast chicken thoroughly at 275 degrees. Gauge the cooking time depending on the cut of the poultry. When it turns very light pink inside, take it out it of the oven and set it aside. The residual heat will finish the cooking and it will be very tender and delicious. To be sure your poultry is cooked to perfection, insert an instant-read thermometer into the thickest part of the meat: properly cooked breast meat is 160 degrees and leg and thigh meat, 175 degrees. Another way to ensure tender chicken is to brine it in saltwater for 45 minutes to an hour before cooking. Brining is a technique that increases the moisture and tenderness of the meat. It's similar to marinating because the meat's cells absorb and retain the water, making it very moist and flavorful when cooked.

Grilling (aka barbecuing) meats is a time-honored cooking method, especially in the U.S. However, you should be aware that high-heat cooking of meats, including frying, forms highly carcinogenic chemicals called heterocyclic amines (HCAs). Luckily, on The Body Ecology Diet there are two ways to combat their effects.

First, marinate your fish, meat, or poultry. A combination of lemon juice, onion, garlic, rosemary, thyme, and dark lager beer is a popular choice. The powerful antioxidants inhibit the formation of HCAs.

Second, eat fermented cruciferous vegetables with your grilled foods. Cruciferous veggies contain sulforaphane (see sidebar), a chemical compound that helps the body detoxify and rid itself of HCAs. Unfortunately, regular cooking methods destroy an important anti-cancer enzyme called myrosinase, a precursor to the production of sulforaphane. The solution? Fermenting! Fermented veggies top the list of HCA-fighting foods. Fermenting cruciferous veggies like kale, cabbage, and broccoli also pre-digests the vegetables and increases the bio-availability of their vitamins and minerals a hundredfold.

Bottom line, both grilled and fried foods contain dangerous HCAs and if you want to live a longer, healthier life it's best to eliminate all fried foods from your diet. But if you love grilling, do it from time to time but always marinate the meat, fish, or poultry before putting it on the fire and be sure that fermented veggies are part of your meal.

The Japanese eat raw fish as a staple of their diet and in recent years sushi and sashimi have become very popular here in the U.S. Raw fish is much easier to digest than cooked fish, so you're actually obtaining more bio-available protein. To kill any parasites or bacteria, freeze raw fish for a minimum of 48 hours, then defrost. Slice the fish into small pieces and serve with low-sodium, wheat-free tamari and a delicious bowl of miso soup made with the sea vegetables wakame and kombu. And please don't forget the cultured vegetables.

Eat Your Sulforaphanes!

Sulforaphane, found in cruciferous vegetables, has many benefits in addition to battling HCAs. It has been shown to help control type 2 diabetes, lower cholesterol, and protect the brain from depression. Research has also shown that sulforaphane prevents breast, colon, and prostate cancers, and may even help those suffering from COPD. It can help control H. pylori, which is linked to the development of ulcers and cancer of the stomach. It also expresses a gene called Nrf2, thought by many researchers to be a "master controller of aging."

You can buy sulforaphane as a supplement but it is obviously more delicious to eat the foods that provide it! Broccoli has the most, but broccoli seeds are an even richer source. So pile on the cruciferous vegetables and be certain to add the fermented veggies whenever you serve grilled meats.

Braised Lamb Shanks

Ingredients:

2 teaspoons unfiltered olive oil or coconut oil

2 lamb shanks, 1 pound each

1 yellow onion, coarsely chopped

2 to 3 cups of non-starchy vegetables, chopped

1 teaspoon sea salt

1 teaspoon dried rosemary

½ teaspoon dried thyme

1 bay leaf

Several pinches of cayenne pepper

¼ cup of red wine or chicken broth (both optional)

Enough water to cover lamb and vegetables

Several sprigs of fresh mint

Stone-ground mustard

Directions:

1. Put olive oil in pot and sauté the lamb over low heat until browned.

2. Remove the lamb shanks and set aside.

3. Add onions to the pot and sauté until just translucent.

4. Return lamb shanks to the pot and arrange vegetables evenly around them.

5. Combine sea salt, herbs, cayenne, and the liquids and pour over the lamb and vegetables.

6. Lay mint sprigs on top.

7. Cover, reduce heat to low, and simmer until lamb is fork tender, approximately 3 hours.

8. Serve with stone-ground mustard.

Lamb shanks can be prepared in a slow cooker or in a roasting pan in the oven. Enameled cast iron cookware works nicely because it can go from cooktop to oven. Buy grass-fed lamb whenever possible.

Beef and Broccoli with Shirataki

Ingredients:

1 pound tender beef steak

1 package konjac shirataki noodles

1 pound fresh broccoli florets, cut into 1-inch pieces

2 tablespoons olive oil

¼ cup scallions, minced

3 cloves garlic, minced

1 tablespoon fresh ginger, minced

1 teaspoon wasabi powder or Chinese five spice

1 teaspoon wheat-free tamari

Herbamare, if desired

Directions:

1. Grill or broil steak until medium rare. Cut into thin strips and set aside.

2. Cook shirataki noodles according to package directions. Drain and set aside.

3. Steam broccoli until tender. Drain well and set aside.

4. Sauté the garlic and scallions in olive oil in a large skillet until soft.

5. Dissolve wasabi in the tamari, add ginger, and stir into the garlic and scallions.

6. Add the shirataki noodles, beef, and broccoli and toss until combined. Season with Herbamare if desired.

Slow Cooker Vegetable Beef or Lamb Stew

■ ■ □ ■ □ ■ ■

Ingredients:

1½ pounds daikon, cut into wedges

1 strip of kombu

3 tablespoons olive oil

1 pound beef chuck stew meat *or* lamb, cut into 1-inch cubes

¼ teaspoon Celtic sea salt

4 to 6 dried shiitake mushrooms, soaked, stemmed, halved

4 carrots, cut into ¾-inch wedges

1 bag frozen pearl onions

6 garlic cloves, sliced

3 tablespoons reduced-sodium tamari

¼ cup red wine vinegar

½ cup red wine (optional)

Directions:

1. Place daikon wedges and a strip kombu in the slow cooker.

2. Heat a large skillet over medium-high heat and add olive oil then beef or lamb and salt. Turn until all sides are browned. Remove meat with a slotted spoon and add to the slower cooker.

3. Add mushrooms to the skillet and cook, stirring frequently and adding a bit of water if necessary, until mushrooms brown. Place in the slow cooker.

4. Add carrots, onions and garlic to the slow cooker

5. Whisk together tamari, vinegar and red wine in a small bowl and pour over the vegetables. (The alcohol in the wine will cook off.)

6. Add enough water so that it is two inches above the food.

7. Cover and cook until meat is very tender, approximately 8 to 10 hours on low or 4 to 5 hours on high.

8. Add sea salt, Herbamare, or other herbs or seasonings to taste, and serve.

Turkey Lettuce Wraps

■ ■ □ ■ ■ ■ ■

Ingredients:

2 cups cooked turkey, finely diced

2 tablespoons onion, chopped

¼ cup celery, chopped

2 teaspoons fresh tarragon, chopped

Apple Cider Vinaigrette, to taste (page 95)

Romaine lettuce leaves

Pumpkin seed oil

Directions:

1. Combine all ingredients and serve rolled in romaine lettuce leaves.

2. For an exceptional taste sensation, drizzle some pumpkin seed oil on your wrap before eating.

This is the perfect healthy recipe to use those leftovers after your Thanksgiving meal!

Body Ecology Turkey Loaf

Ingredients:

1 pound ground turkey

1 egg

2 carrots, finely chopped

1 small zucchini, chopped

1 large onion, finely chopped

1 large red pepper, diced fine

1½ stalks celery, finely chopped

1 tablespoon Worcestershire sauce
   (The Wizard's™ gluten-free)

½ teaspoon Celtic sea salt

1 tablespoon whole grain mustard

½ teaspoon garlic powder

2 tablespoons parsley flakes

Directions:

1. Preheat oven to 350 degrees.

2. Combine all ingredients and mold into loaf pan.

3. Bake for 1 hour.

Turkey Burgers with Sweet Mustard Sauce

Ingredients:

4 tablespoons Dijon-style mustard

1 teaspoon dry mustard

8 to 10 drops Body Ecology's stevia liquid
   concentrate

2 tablespoons raw, organic apple cider
   vinegar

½ cup organic, unfiltered olive oil, liquefied
   coconut oil or liquefied ghee

½ cup chopped fresh dill or 1 teaspoon
   dried dill

1 pound ground turkey (preferably dark
   meat)

2 teaspoons Celtic sea salt

2 tablespoons coconut oil, divided

Directions:

1. Make the sauce first so that the flavors will have time to blend. Combine the mustard, dry mustard, stevia and vinegar in a medium-size bowl. Whisk in the oil until the sauce is thick and well blended. Stir in the dill. Set aside and let rest for at least one hour.

2. Mix the ground turkey, 1 tablespoon coconut oil, and sea salt well and form into four patties.

3. Heat the remaining 1 tablespoon coconut oil in a large skillet over a low flame. Add the patties and cook for 5 to 7 minutes. Turn and continue to cook until they medium rare inside.

4. Serve the burgers hot with a dollop of the sweet mustard sauce, either atop your favorite salad greens or accompanied by non-starchy vegetables like green beans or broccolini.

When these juicy no-bun burgers are made with dark turkey meat they have more natural fatty acids than those made with white meat.

Zucchini Boats with Savory Turkey Stuffing ■ ■ ■ ■ ■ ■ ■

Ingredients:

4 zucchini cut in half lengthwise, trimmed, cleaned, blanched

3 cloves garlic, minced

1 small onion, minced

2 stalks celery, minced

3 tablespoons fresh parsley, chopped

1 teaspoon oregano

1 teaspoon paprika

½ teaspoon fresh pepper

¼ teaspoon cayenne pepper

¼ teaspoon Celtic sea salt

1 pound ground turkey

2 eggs, scrambled

2 to 3 tablespoon coconut oil

Directions:

1. Preheat oven to 375 degrees.

2. Scoop out centers of zucchini, taking care not to pierce skins.

3. Sauté onion, garlic and celery together in large skillet until the onion is translucent.

4. Add seasonings and sea salt and sauté a few minutes more. Add the ground turkey and scrambled eggs and remove from heat.

5. Stuff each zucchini boat with vegetable/turkey mixture and place in a deep-sided roasting dish.

6. Bake for 30 minutes or until turkey is slightly golden on top and cooked throughout.

Chicken Breasts Roasted in Fresh Garden Herbs ■ ■ ■ ■

Ingredients:

1 cup fresh oregano leaves

1 cup scallions, coarsely chopped

4 tablespoons fresh cilantro, coarsely chopped

2 small garlic cloves

Juice of 2 lemons

1 tablespoon melted coconut oil or ghee

1 teaspoon fine-grind Celtic sea salt

½ teaspoon crushed red pepper flakes

4 free-range, organic boneless, skinless chicken breasts

Directions:

1. Combine all ingredients except chicken breasts in a food processor bowl and process until minced.

2. Place chicken in a casserole dish, top evenly with the herb mixture and marinate, refrigerated, for at least one hour.

3. Roast very slowly at 275 degrees for one hour and 15 minutes, or until the chicken breasts are very pale pink. (About 170 degrees on an instant-read thermometer).

Turkey Cabbage Rolls

Ingredients:

1 head green cabbage

1½ teaspoons whole mustard seed

½ teaspoon whole celery seed

¼ teaspoon dried rosemary

1 pound ground turkey

½ large zucchini, finely shredded

½ large carrot, finely shredded

½ large red bell pepper, diced

½ large white onion, diced large

½ serrano chile, minced

1 clove garlic, minced or smashed

½ bunch parsley, roughly chopped

1½ teaspoon Celtic sea salt

2 ounces melted coconut oil

This is an all-around great recipe—easy to prepare and easily adapted to your taste, budget, and the contents of your fridge. You can double the recipe and freeze the leftovers! These little rolls are great to serve at dinner parties—make a batch a day ahead and refrigerate until ready to cook using any of the methods listed. It just might become your signature dish!

Directions:

1. Cut the cabbage stem flush with the head. Carefully peel off as many whole leaves as desired, cutting back the stem as needed.

2. Set a large stockpot of water to boil and put a colander in the sink.

3. Immerse 3 or 4 cabbage leaves for 1 to 2 minutes in boiling water until just flexible. Remove with tongs and place in the colander to cool and drain.

4. Toast rosemary, mustard, and celery seeds in a small dry skillet until fragrant. When mustard seeds just begin to pop, remove from heat. Cool for 5 minutes then roughly grind them. Place in a large mixing bowl.

5. Add turkey, zucchini, carrot, onion, bell peppers, onion, chile, garlic, parsley, celery and sea salt to the seed mixture. Pour in the coconut oil, and using your hands or a large spoon mix until ingredients are evenly distributed.

6. Put a large scoop of filling inside a cabbage leaf (natural curl up). Starting with the stem end, roll up like a burrito, folding the sides in as you roll to seal.

7. Place rolls, seam down, on a tray or in a baking dish Cook immediately or refrigerate/freeze for later use.

8. Here are some suggested cooking methods:

   - Steaming. Pour about 3 to 4 cups of your favorite broth or stock into a pot with a steaming basket. Add cabbage rolls in a single layer. Bring to a boil and allow the rolls to steam for 5 minutes. Turn with tongs and steam for 5 minutes, or until cooked through.

   - Baking. Arrange cabbage rolls in a single layer in a baking dish. Add just enough broth (page 57) or gravy (page 111) to fill the space between the rolls. Cover and bake at 350 degrees for 35 to 40 minutes.

   - Slow cooking. Fill slow cooker with cabbage rolls, seam side down. Add enough broth to fill half way. Cook for 8 hours on low.

9. Cabbage rolls should reach 165 degrees on an instant-read thermometer before serving.

Quick and Easy Pan Roasted Chicken and Veggies ▪ ▪ ▪

Ingredients:

2 chicken breasts, bone-in, cut in half
  crosswise

2 chicken drumsticks, skinless

2 chicken thighs, skinless

12 small Brussels sprouts, trimmed, halved

6 shallots, peeled, halved

6 cloves of garlic, peeled

1 red bell pepper, cut into 8 pieces

3 small, slender daikon, cut into 1-inch
  pieces

4 teaspoons fresh thyme, minced, divided

2 teaspoons fresh rosemary, minced, divided

2 teaspoons fresh marjoram, minced, divided

2 tablespoons extra virgin olive oil

1 teaspoon Celtic sea salt and/or Herbamare

2 tablespoons ghee, melted

Directions:

1. Preheat oven to 350 degrees.

2. Wash chicken pieces and pat dry.

3. Toss all veggies, half of the fresh herbs, and ½ teaspoon salt or Herbamare with the olive oil in a large bowl.

4. Arrange vegetables in a single layer on a rimmed baking sheet and top with the chicken.

5. Combine ghee with the remaining herbs and sea salt. Spoon the mixture over the chicken.

6. Place the baking sheet on the upper middle oven rack and roast for approximately 40 minutes or until the breast meat reaches 160 degrees and the thighs and drumsticks register 175 degrees using an instant-read thermometer.

7. Remove chicken from oven and let rest, covered in parchment paper, for 10 minutes before serving.

Aromatic Roasted Game Hens ▪ ▪ ▪ ▪ ▪ ▪ ▪

Ingredients:

4 game hens, thawed

2 teaspoons ground coriander

2 teaspoons cumin

1 teaspoon turmeric

1 teaspoon Celtic sea salt

1 to 2 tablespoons ghee

Directions:

1. Preheat oven to 350 degrees.

2. Wash and pat hens dry.

3. Mix all dry ingredients and divide in half.

4. Gently rub half of the dry ingredients between the skin and meat of hens.

5. Baste the hens with ghee and coat the birds generously with the remaining dry rub.

6. Bake uncovered for 1 hour, or until juices run clear and the thigh meat registers 160 degrees on an instant-read thermometer.

Spicy Roasted Game Hens

Ingredients:

2 game hens, skin removed

1 tablespoon fresh ginger

2 large garlic cloves

1 tablespoon fresh lemon juice

½ cup olive oil

2 teaspoons paprika

2 teaspoons cumin

½ teaspoon turmeric

¼ teaspoon cayenne pepper

¼ teaspoon cinnamon

Pinch nutmeg

Pinch cloves

Celtic sea salt, to taste

Directions:

1. Preheat oven to 350 degrees.

2. Wash and pat hens dry.

3. Purée ginger and garlic in food processor. Add remaining ingredients and process until smooth.

4. Place hens in large bowl. Massage the hens, inside and out with some of the marinade. Cover and refrigerate for 4 to 6 hours.

5. Place hens breast side up on a rack in a shallow roasting pan. Spoon the rest of the marinade over hens.

6. Roast, uncovered for 50 to 60 minutes, or until the thigh meat registers 160 degrees on an instant-read thermometer. (Insert thermometer in the inner thigh area near the breast but not touching bone.)

Grilled Tuna and Red Onions

Ingredients:

1 large red onion

1½ quarts filtered water

2 teaspoons Celtic sea salt, divided

2 tablespoons raw, organic apple cider vinegar

4 tablespoons coconut oil or ghee

12 ounces fresh tuna, cut to 1-inch strips

Juice of 1 lemon

2 tablespoons fresh parsley

2 tablespoons fresh cilantro

Directions:

1. Slice red onions into approximately 16 rings. Bring water to a boil with ½ teaspoon of the sea salt. Add onions and blanch for 2 minutes. Drain and transfer onions to a bowl.

2. While onions are still hot, add the vinegar, coconut oil or ghee, and ½ teaspoon of sea salt.

3. Heat up the grill.

4. Lightly oil the tuna on both sides and sprinkle with ½ teaspoon of sea salt. Grill until medium-rare, about 2 minutes per side. Let cool, then break into 1-inch chunks.

5. Gently combine tuna chunks, lemon juice, remaining ½ teaspoon of sea salt, and parsley with the pickled onions. Allow to marinate for 1 hour. Stir in the fresh cilantro and serve at room temperature.

Red Trout with Asparagus ■ ■ ■ ■ ■ ■ ■ ■

Ingredients:

1 pound pencil-thin asparagus

1½ pounds red trout fillets

2 tablespoons coconut oil, melted

2 tablespoons freshly squeezed lemon juice, divided

½ teaspoon Celtic sea salt, or to taste

Cayenne pepper, to taste

2 scallions, chopped

2 tablespoons water

½ cup fresh parsley, chopped

Lemon wedges

Directions:

1. Cut asparagus spears into thirds. Blanch, shock in cold water, and set aside.

2. Preheat oven to 375 degrees.

3. Place fish in a baking dish. Pour coconut oil over fish and turn to coat. Sprinkle with 1 tablespoon lemon juice, sea salt, cayenne pepper, and scallions. Add 2 tablespoons water.

4. Bake uncovered for 7 minutes.

5. Arrange asparagus around fish. Cover and bake for an additional 5 minutes.

6. Combine remaining 1 tablespoon lemon juice and parsley and sprinkle over fish. Serve with lemon wedges.

Salmon Cakes on Spinach or Kale ■ ■ ■ ■ ■ ■ ■ ■

Ingredients:

1 pound salmon fillets, skin removed

½ of a small red onion

1 tablespoon dried dill

1 tablespoon Worcestershire sauce (The Wizard's™ gluten-free)

¼ teaspoon cayenne pepper

2 teaspoons Celtic sea salt

Herbamare to taste

2 tablespoons ghee, divided

2 pounds fresh spinach *or* kale

Directions:

1. Pulse red onion in food processor until finely diced. Transfer to a large bowl.

2. Add salmon, several chunks at a time, pulsing quickly to create a roughly ground consistency. Avoid over-processing.

3. Combine salmon with onion and add remaining ingredients except ghee. Gently combine mixture with your hands and form into patties.

4. Heat 1 tablespoon ghee in a skillet. Cook patties for a few minutes on each side.

5. Sauté spinach in 1 tablespoon ghee over low heat, just until soft and wilted. Sprinkle with sea salt to taste (or sauté kale in olive oil until tender.)

6. Serve salmon patties on the wilted spinach (or kale).

This recipe is also excellent served with other greens, such as collards.

Shrimp Ceviche

■ ■ ■ ■ ■ ■ ■

Ingredients:

1 pound of high-quality medium, raw, fresh shrimp

Juice of 6 limes

½ cup freshly squeezed lemon juice

1 cup cucumber, peeled, seeded, finely chopped

1 cup red bell pepper, finely chopped

½ cup scallions, finely chopped

1 small bunch of cilantro

1 small jalapeño, seeded, minced

Pinch of Celtic sea salt, or to taste

Directions:

1. Rinse shrimp and remove tails, peel, and devein. Slice thinly into a glass serving bowl.

2. Cover with lime juice then cover bowl and refrigerate for at least 4 hours. Shrimp will become opaque as the acid in the lime juice "cooks" the shrimp.

3. Combine the remaining ingredients in a separate glass bowl and marinate in the lemon juice

4. Once the shrimp is "cooked" rinse it well and add to marinating vegetables.

Try sole, halibut, sea bass or tilapia instead of shrimp!

Spanish Shrimp

■ ■ ■ ■ ■ ■ ■

Ingredients:

½ pound of fresh or frozen raw shrimp

2 tablespoons of olive oil

½ red onion, sliced into rings

½ yellow onion, sliced into rings

1 teaspoon Worcestershire sauce

1 teaspoon wheat-free tamari

1 pinch of sea salt

1 pinch of Herbamare

Directions:

1. Peel and devein the shrimp.

2. Heat the olive oil in a pan over medium heat. Add the remaining ingredients, except shrimp, and sauté for 5 minutes.

3. Add the shrimp and cook for 3 minutes, stirring often.

Pepper-Grilled Salmon Steaks with Corn Salsa ▪ ▪ ▪ ▪ ▪

Ingredients:

1 can of white corn, drained

1 jalapeño, seeded, chopped

1 large red bell pepper, seeded, chopped

2 tablespoons red onion, finely chopped

1 tablespoon fresh cilantro, finely chopped

2 tablespoons fresh lime juice

4 six-ounce salmon steaks, 1 inch thick

1 teaspoon crushed red pepper flakes

Sea salt, to taste

Directions:

1. Coat grill rack with cooking spray. Preheat grill to medium-high (350 to 400 degrees).

2. Combine corn, jalapeño, bell pepper, onion, cilantro, and lime juice in a bowl and set aside.

3. Sprinkle the salmon with red pepper flakes and sea salt.

4. Grill salmon for 3 or 4 minutes on each side, turning once.

5. Top with corn salsa and serve.

Cedar Plank Cod with Cilantro ▪ ▪ ▪ ▪ ▪ ▪ ▪ ▪

Ingredients:

Cedar planks, soaked 2 to 6 hours
   (overnight is even better)

4 cod fillets, 5 to 6 ounces each

¼ cup fresh cilantro

½ cup olive oil

1 garlic clove, chopped

Juice of 1 lime

½ teaspoon crushed red pepper flakes

1 teaspoon Lakanto

Filtered water

Celtic sea salt

Directions:

1. Preheat grill to medium-high (350 to 400 degrees). Brush fish with oil and season with sea salt. Place each fillet on a cedar plank.

2. Place planks on the grill. Grill, covered, for about 10 to 12 minutes or until fish flakes easily with a fork.

3. Purée cilantro, oil, garlic, lime juice, red pepper flakes, Lakanto, and 1 tablespoon hot water in a blender until smooth.

4. Spoon the cilantro sauce over fillets and serve.

Using a Thermometer

When cooking meat, the use of a thermometer is highly recommended. There are several types available. The classic meat thermometer is inserted in the meat and left in place during cooking. Instant-read thermometers can be used to determine food temperatures quickly during any stage of cooking. Both analog and digital types are available. Choose a thermometer that suits your style of cooking and follow the manufacturer's directions to ensure food safety and the most flavorful meats. Be sure that your thermometer is for meat and not for candy or appliances.

Sautéed Barramundi

■ ■ ■ ■ ■

Ingredients:

2 teaspoons fennel seed

1 teaspoon cumin seed

1 tablespoon fresh thyme leaves

1 teaspoon Lakanto

¼ teaspoon Celtic sea salt or Herbamare to taste

1 pound barramundi fillets

2 eggs, beaten

2 teaspoons olive oil

Directions:

1. Heat a small skillet over medium heat. Add fennel and cumin seeds and cook for about 1 minute or just until aromatic and lightly toasted. Shake pan occasionally to avoid burning.

2. Remove from heat and stir in thyme leaves. Transfer mixture to a small reusable plastic bag.

3. Add Lakanto and sea salt. Using a rolling pin or mallet, crush spices until coarse. Set aside.

4. Rinse barramundi fillets and pat dry with paper towels. Dip in beaten egg and coat both sides of each fillet with spice mixture, pressing lightly.

5. Sauté for about 3 to 4 minutes or until fish flakes easily with a fork. Serve hot.

Bone Broth

■ ■ ■ ■ ■

Ingredients:

2 pounds assorted bones from free-range, organically raised, grass-fed animals

1 gallon filtered water

2 tablespoons apple cider vinegar or wine

You can save bones from your own kitchen or purchase some from your local butcher. Larger bones should be cut into pieces. Try to use a variety that can offer the benefits of both yellow and red marrow. Yellow marrow is in the center of long bones. It gives fat and flavor. Red marrow is found in flat bones. It provides stem cell factors to boost immunity.

Delicious, mineral-rich bone broth contains collagen to help make your skin supple and reduce cellulite.

Directions:

1. Place bones in a large stockpot and cover with filtered water. Add apple cider vinegar or wine and slowly bring to a boil. Cover and reduce heat to a low simmer.

2. Periodically skim residue from the surface as it rises.

3. Larger bones (beef) can simmer for 12 to 72 hours. Smaller bones (poultry) can cook for 6 to 48 hours.

4. Keep broth covered while cooking. Add water, if necessary.

5. Strain broth and discard bones.

6. Allow to cool then refrigerate for up to 3 days. Retain the fat layer on top until broth is used. The broth can also be frozen.

7. Use as a recipe base or sip as a beverage.

Notes

Notes

Fermented Foods ■ ■ ■ ■ and Probiotic Liquids

Fermentation is one of the oldest ways to preserve food. Refrigeration is only a relatively recent luxury, and for thousands of years humans relied on fermented (also known as cultured) foods through the long winters until they could grow fresh fruits and vegetables again. When we ferment our foods, we purposely expose them to selected probiotic microbes and encourage these microbes to grow by placing the food in a warm or room temperature environment. As microbes feed on the sugars in the food, they break down the plant fibers (cellulose), the proteins and the fats. They also preserve it. In truth, fermented foods are survival food.

Fermented foods and drinks are the "rock stars" of The Body Ecology Diet. The basic recipes for making fermented vegetables, coconut kefir and milk kefir are included here but you'll find even more information on fermented foods and drinks at www.bodyecology.com. Because they are so vital in your journey toward health and healing we encourage you to learn more. Our hope is that you'll become familiar with making them (it's easy!) and begin to enjoy them with each and every meal.

The fermented-food recipes that we are focusing on in this cookbook are:

- Raw fermented vegetables and lacto-fermented pickles
- Fermented coconut water kefir
- Raw dairy kefir for those who can digest dairy

Other fermented foods that we at Body Ecology can recommend are:

- Our probiotic liquids grown on seeds and grains (InnergyBiotic™ and Cocobiotic™)
- Our fermented protein powders with microalgae, such as spirulina, and cereal grasses, as a source of vegan protein (SuperSpirulina Plus™ and Vitality SuperGreen™)
- Traditional fermented soy-based foods such as miso, natto and tempeh
- Traditional fermented dairy, such as homemade yogurt, raw cheese, and sour cream

Be sure to check the labels for live probiotic value if you are purchasing any fermented foods from a store.

Fermented foods are pre-digested by bacteria and yeast, making their nutrients easier for the gut to break down and absorb. The standard American diet, which tends toward high-carbohydrate, acidic, mineral-deficient, processed foods made with bad fats, combined with the effects of aging and constant high levels of stress, have left many people without enough gastric acid or pancreatic enzymes. Because probiotic and enzyme-rich fermented foods are pre-digested, it means less work for your stomach and your small intestine. Eating fermented vegetables with a meal helps with digestion of the entire meal.

As friendly bacteria consume the sugars that are naturally found in raw vegetables, fruits and dairy foods, they produce lactic acid, which contributes to the sour taste of fermented foods. Lactic acid released into the gut controls intestinal candida overgrowth. Research also shows that the lactic-acid bacteria in fermented foods stop intestinal inflammation and helps heal a permeable gut lining.

Cultured vegetables, young coconut kefir and the other fermented foods we recommend will become important tools in your journey toward healing.

Fermented foods have a long list of benefits. They support healthy digestion. They help balance your immune system and can play a very important role in detoxification. They contribute to brain health and support positive mental and emotional well-being. They have long been credited for helping those who eat them live longer, healthier happier lives.

First Try This

Taking probiotic supplements has become very trendy. They are certainly of great value, but we suggest adding fermented foods to your diet even before taking a probiotic supplement. The hardier beneficial microbes in fermented foods are well equipped to set up residence in your digestive tract and change the environment of your intestines. They help create the right balance of microbes and clear the way for the more fragile probiotics to thrive there. In the inner ecosystem, it's all about balance.

HOMEMADE FERMENTED VEGETABLES

The key to making a successful batch of beautiful, brightly colored cultured veggies is to use freshly harvested, organic vegetables. Wash them thoroughly and blot off excess water. Clean equipment is essential! Scald everything you use in very hot water.

Vegetables can be cut by hand or with a mandoline but a food processor is much faster and works well for firm vegetables like cabbage, carrots, daikon, onions, etc.

Basic Recipe for Fermented Vegetables ▪ ▪ ▪ ▪ ▪

How to Make Fermented Vegetables. *Use this easy method and the microbial-enriched brine to make all of the fermented veggie recipes in this section.*

1. Choose one of the fermented veggie recipes below.
2. Combine all cut or shredded veggies in a large mixing bowl.
3. Add brine (see below) to veggie mixture, mixing well.
4. Pack vegetables into 1-quart wide-mouth Mason jars, leaving about 2 inches of space at the top so that veggies can expand. Push down on veggies as if you were attempting to push all the air out of the jar.
5. Roll up several reserved cabbage leaves into a tight "logs" and fit into the top of each jar to fill the space. Place lid on each jar. While fermenting, the vegetables should always be under the liquid brine. If you need to add more liquid to your shredded vegetables once they are packed into the jars just add a little more filtered water.
6. Let veggies sit for 7 days at room temperature (70 to 72 degrees). You can refrigerate the jars to slow down fermentation.
7. Enjoy with each meal!

How to Make Microbial-Enriched Brine

Ingredients:

3 red apples, chopped

2 teaspoons Celtic sea salt

1 teaspoon Body Ecology EcoBloom powder

1 packet of Body Ecology Culture Starter

Body Ecology Ancient Earth Minerals (contents of 6 capsules)

4 cups water

Directions:

Put all the ingredients into a high-speed blender and blend well.

This recipe makes enough brine for approximately nine 1-quart jars of cultured vegetables.

Version 1 Ingredients:

3 heads green cabbage, shredded, reserving 5 or 6 whole, large leaves

1 bunch kale, chopped by hand

½ cup to 1 cup wakame, cut into pieces with kitchen shears

1 tablespoon dill seed

2 teaspoons Celtic sea salt

Microbial-enriched brine (page 173)

Version 2 Ingredients:

3 heads green cabbage, shredded, reserving 5 or 6 whole, large leaves

6 large carrots, shredded

1 3-inch piece ginger, peeled, chopped

6 cloves garlic, peeled, chopped

2 teaspoons Celtic sea salt

Microbial-enriched brine (page 173)

Spicy Red Blend ■ ■ ■ ■ ■

Ingredients:

3 heads red cabbage, shredded in food processor, reserving 5 or 6 whole, large leaves

2 red onions, sliced thin and then coarsely chopped or shredded in food processor

1 large bunch fresh cilantro, rinsed, coarsely chopped

2 medium red bell peppers, diced by hand

4 to 6 cloves garlic, chopped

1 large poblano chile, de-stemmed, sliced (more seeds equal more heat)

2 carrots, shredded in food processor

Microbial-enriched brine (page 173)

Green Cabbage, Kale, Onion and Fennel Blend ■ ■ ■ ■ ■

Ingredients:

3 heads of green cabbage, shredded, reserving 5 or 6 whole, large leaves.

1 large bunch kale, chopped by hand

1 large bunch fresh mint, coarsely chopped by hand

1 large fennel bulb, shredded in food processor

2 yellow or sweet onions, sliced thin or shredded in food processor

Microbial-enriched brine (page 173)

Storage and Safety

Fermented vegetables will be safe to eat for up to one year but they will continue to become more and more sour. They also won't have as many live beneficial bacteria after about 2 months.

Dilly Green Blend

■ ■ ■ ■ ■

Ingredients:

3 heads green cabbage, shredded, reserving 5
or 6 whole, large leaves

3 large cucumbers, cut into thin slices by hand

Bunch fresh dill, coarsely chopped

2 yellow or sweet Vidalia onions, sliced thin or
shredded in food processor

1 tablespoon dill seed

4 large cloves garlic (optional)

¼ cup dried, cut wakame (soaked in water
for 10 minutes to soften)

Microbial-enriched brine (page 173)

Body Ecology's Version of Classic Kimchi

■ ■ ■ ■ ■

Ingredients:

1 head napa cabbage, approximately 2½ to 3
pounds, coarsely chopped, reserving 5 or 6
whole, large leaves

1 medium daikon radish, shredded in food
processor or cut into ¼ inch cubes

3 carrots, shredded in food processor

4 scallions, cut into 1-inch pieces

4 cloves of garlic, finely diced

4 tablespoons fresh ginger, finely minced

2 tablespoons chili powder

Microbial-enriched brine (page 173)

Quick and Easy Homemade Dill Pickles

■ ■ ■ ■ ■

Ingredients:

4 small, unpeeled pickling cucumbers,
quartered lengthwise

2 cloves of garlic

4 pearl onions, sliced in half

2 sprigs of fresh dill

½ tsp coriander seeds

¼ tsp mustard seeds

¼ tsp whole peppercorns

2 cups of water

1 tablespoon coarse, grey Celtic sea salt

1 thick slice from a large onion

Directions:

1. Pack cucumber slices, garlic and pearl onions tightly into a 1-quart glass jar.

2. Add the herbs and spices on top.

3. Combine the water and sea salt to make a brine.

4. Pour brine into the jar, leaving about an inch of space.

5. Place the thick onion slice on top to completely submerge the ingredients in the jar. You can also use rolled up cabbage or kale leaves.

6. Seal the jar and let pickles sit at room temperature for 3 days. If after 3 days the pickles are not yet to your taste, let them sit for another day or two. You still want them to have some crunch. Refrigerate when they're the way you like them.

Kefir is a cultured and microbial-rich food that helps restore your inner ecology. Its beneficial strains of bacteria and yeasts maintain a symbiotic relationship that gives kefir antibiotic properties. Both coconut kefir and milk kefir share the same strains of beneficial bacteria and yeast but, of course, one is made from milk and the other from coconut water.

Either can be made with "grains" or a culture starter. We have found that a starter is more convenient because once the kefir is made the grains must be removed from the milk or the coconut water and transferred in order to start the next batch. In between uses, the grains must be stored in fresh milk to survive and if you travel or don't use them within a week the bacteria will die off without a fresh supply of milk or coconut water to feed upon. As they are transferred from batch to batch the grains can also be easily contaminated. However, if you make large batches of kefir it is more economical to purchase grains online.

Young Coconut Kefir

Young coconut kefir is an important probiotic, alkalizing and mineral-rich fermented food. You should begin drinking it in Stage 1 of The Body Ecology Diet. You'll soon find that with its abundance of exceptionally powerful and beneficial microbiota, it will help you to quickly establish your inner ecosystem. Young coconut kefir and coconut kefir cheese have no casein. They introduce dairy-loving bacteria into the intestines so that if you eventually choose to drink kefir made from milk, you'll have a much better chance of tolerating it—if it's introduced slowly and in small amounts.

Ingredients:

1½ quarts of water from approximately 3 young coconuts

Body Ecology's Kefir Starter and/or Veggie Culture Starter

Directions:

1. Extract the water from several young coconuts using the method on page 177.

2. Pour the coconut water into a saucepan and heat to 92 degrees. Use a cooking thermometer to check the temperature, or wash your hands well and dip your finger into the coconut water to test. At 92 degrees, it won't feel either hot or cold, much the same as testing baby formula. Do not overheat! A temperature above 105 degrees will kill the microbiota and most of the enzymes and vitamins will be destroyed.

3. Add 1 packet of Body Ecology's Kefir Starter to the warmed coconut water. The Kefir Starter contains different strains of Lactobacillus as well as beneficial yeast. (Body Ecology's Veggie Culture Starter can be used instead of the kefir starter or in addition to the kefir starter to add L. plantarum, a very beneficial bacterium that makes folate.)

4. Pour coconut water with starter into a glass container with tight-fitting lid. (The water from three coconuts will usually fill a 1.5 quart jar.) Tighten the lid on the jar and shake vigorously.

5. Ferment the coconut water at 72 to75 degrees for 36 hours. Insulate if necessary to maintain this consistent temperature. Maintaining this temperature is essential for a successful batch.

6. Save enough coconut milk kefir from this batch to begin your next batch. Instructions are on page 183.

Young coconut kefir is a discovery unique to Body Ecology. It quickly became one of our favorite medicinal drinks! It stops cravings for sugar, aids in the digestion of all foods, while toning and cleansing the intestines and the liver. We've had many reports of it easing aches and joint pains, clearing up skin problems, improving vision, making hair and nails healthier because of its high mineral content (potassium, natural sodium, and chloride), and helping to cleanse the endocrine system (adrenals, thyroid, pituitary, ovaries).

Coconut water kefir does not thicken like milk kefir. It is ready when it becomes cloudy and an effervescent layer forms on the top. The taste is slightly tart and tangy, while some of the original sweetness remains.

How to Choose a Coconut

Choose young coconuts with unblemished white husks free of mold. The husk covers a thinner brown fibrous shell. Inside that shell is a thin, pliable layer of meat called "spoon meat." The center of the young coconut is full of water.

How to Open a Coconut

TO REMOVE THE COCONUT WATER: Lay the coconut on its side. Cut several thin slices from the bottom of the husk until you see a white or brown ring. Set the opposite end in your sink drain to hold the coconut steady. Find the soft spot inside the ring. (If there's a knot, the soft spot is usually in or beside it.) Pierce the soft spot with a clean screwdriver. Widen the hole with a vegetable peeler, if necessary. Pour the water into a measuring cup or glass jar. The water should be clear or slightly cloudy. If it's pink or purple, some people say it is safe to eat, but we prefer not to use it.

TO EXTRACT THE COCONUT MEAT: After the coconut water is removed, lay the nut on its side on a solid surface. Strike the coconut in the center with one strong stroke using a cleaver or knife. If the coconut doesn't split open, tap the cleaver blade with a mallet until it does. (If this doesn't work well for you, you can find other methods on the internet.) If the spoon meat is not white, discard it. Scoop the meat from the coconut with a flexible spatula or spoon. Rinse the spoon meat to remove any flecks of shell or fibers.

Coconut Kefir "Cheese"   ■ ■ ■ ■ ■

Ingredients:

Spoon meat from 3 young Thai coconuts

Water, coconut water *or* sour fruit juice

Fresh sour fruit or vanilla beans (optional)

Body Ecology Kefir Starter

Body Ecology EcoBloom (optional)

There is not as much sugar in coconut spoon meat as there is in the coconut water, so it does not need a long fermentation. The longer it ferments the more sour it will become. If your desire is to create a dessert or special treat, 8 hours is ideal.

When your cheese is done, you can purée flavorings like fresh vanilla bean or fresh or frozen berries into the spoon meat. To sweeten, just add Body Ecology's liquid stevia concentrate to taste.

Directions:

1. Place spoon meat (see sidebar on page 177) in a blender or food processor. Add enough water, coconut water or a diluted fruit juice and purée until it's the consistency of a creamy pudding. (Recommended sour fruit juices are pomegranate, blueberry or cherry.)

2. Dissolve the kefir starter in warm water. If desired, add a pinch of EcoBloom, especially if you are using tap water or filtered water. (EcoBloom acts as a prebiotic to fuel the growth of beneficial bacteria.)

3. Divide pudding between two 1-quart glass containers until half full to leave room for the pudding to expand as it ferments.

5. Put an airtight lid onto the container and allow the cheese to ferment for about 8 hours. Refrigerate to stop fermentation.

6. Use the kefir "cheese" in recipes or eat as-is.

Traditional Milk Kefir

■ ■ ■ ■ ■

Kefir from milk is a complete protein with all the essential amino acids. It's a natural antibiotic—and it's delicious! The finished product is not unlike that of a drinking-style yogurt, but kefir has a more tart, refreshing taste and more beneficial bacteria. It also contains strains of beneficial yeast, and yogurt does not.

The Body Ecology Diet generally recommends avoiding dairy products in Stage 1 because milk contains a mucus-forming sugar called lactose that feeds yeast. Because it is fermented, however, milk kefir does not feed yeast, and it usually doesn't even bother people who are lactose intolerant. The friendly bacteria and the beneficial yeast growing in the milk kefir consume most of the lactose and provide very efficient enzymes (lactase) for consuming whatever lactose is still left after the culturing process. Yes, kefir is mucus-forming, but only slightly, if you follow some simple food-combining rules (page 182).

And here's the best part: the slightly mucus-forming quality is exactly what makes milk kefir work for many of us. The mucus has a "clean" quality to it that coats the lining of the digestive tract, creating a sort of nest where beneficial bacteria can settle and colonize. This makes the other probiotics you may be taking even more potent; they now have a better chance to take hold and proliferate in your intestines.

Is Milk Kefir Right for You?

Some people thrive on milk kefir right from the start and others may need to proceed more slowly. People with candidiasis often have a leaky, permeable gut lining. This lining must be healed before you can start drinking kefir made from dairy. It's essential that the protein in milk kefir (casein) does not leak through the gut lining and cause further problems, including allergies.

Once your leaky, permeable gut has healed (12 to 16 weeks on The Diet), you may be able to drink milk kefir. Start with about four ounces in the morning on an empty stomach but dilute it with water, or better yet, a few ounces of CocoBiotic™ or InnergyBiotic™. Every week increase the amount until you are able to drink more, but ideally 4 ounces is enough each day. Children can have more. Think of clever ways to use those 4 to 6 ounces. For instance, you can add it to your morning smoothie or whip some fresh or dried herbs into the kefir to make a dip for raw vegetables. It's also delicious as the base for a salad dressing.

The Benefits of Milk Kefir for All Ages

Milk kefir is an excellent food for children of all ages as long as they do well on dairy. In fact, in Russia milk kefir (diluted with water) was traditionally introduced to babies at the age of 4 months to build their immune systems and enhance breast milk feedings. This is thought to be one of the reasons why Russians are some of the healthiest people in the world.

Who else does well on fermented milk kefir?

- Pre-schoolers and elementary school kids who need a perfect morning protein meal before daycare or class.

- The elderly who suffer from sarcopenia (loss of muscle mass) and who tend to be severely undernourished because of poor digestion.

- Certainly body builders. Milk kefir smoothies make a perfect base for the popular whey protein concentrates that body builders love.

- High school and college students who often eat poorly and whose grades suffer as a result will find milk kefir a very nutritious addition to their daily diet. Kefir is a "brain food." It provides a complete source of protein to jumpstart their brains before classes.

Fermented milk kefir is *not* recommended for people who are casein-intolerant.

Nutritional Benefits of Milk Kefir

Milk kefir is an excellent source of calcium and magnesium for building strong bones. Tryptophan, an essential amino acid found in milk kefir, combines with the calcium and magnesium to help calm the nervous system. Some people call kefir "Nature's tranquilizer." Its calming effect is great for people who are high-strung or nervous, for hyperactive children, or for people with sleep disorders, such as the elderly. The body converts tryptophan into serotonin, an important chemical called a neurotransmitter; balanced serotonin levels can help depression and relieve constipation, induce sleep, and inhibit waking during the night. This conversion is helped along by Vitamin B6, which is also abundant in kefir.

Kefir also has ample phosphorus, the second most abundant mineral in our bodies. Phosphorus is important in utilizing carbohydrates, fats, and proteins for growth, cell maintenance, and energy. A phosphorous deficiency can result in the loss of appetite.

People with digestive problems (and also with candidiasis) are usually deficient in the B vitamins and in Vitamin K because they lack the beneficial bacteria in the intestinal tract that would normally produce them. When kefir is included in the diet, the bacteria and beneficial yeast should soon be able to manufacture sufficient amounts of these much-needed vitamins. Vitamin K promotes blood clotting, encourages the flow of urine, relieves menstrual cramps, increases vitality and longevity, and enhances liver functioning.

Kefir provides biotin, another B vitamin that is missing in people with candidiasis. Biotin is a coenzyme that assists in the manufacture of fatty acids and in the oxidation of fatty acids and carbohydrates. Without biotin, the body's production of essential fatty acids is impaired. Biotin also aids in the body's assimilation of protein and other B vitamins: folic acid, pantothenic acid, and B12. A deficiency of biotin can cause muscular pain, poor appetite, dry skin, lack of energy, depression and a distressed nervous system.

Kefir is an excellent source of Vitamin B12, which is essential for longevity. It is the only vitamin that contains essential mineral elements. It cannot be made synthetically but must be grown, like penicillin, in bacteria or molds. B12 is necessary for the normal metabolism of nerve tissue and for red blood cell formation. B12 builds immunity and can increase energy and counteract allergens. It is also required for normal growth and is important for fertility and during pregnancy. Additionally, it works with folate, another member of the B-complex, in facilitating the synthesis of choline, a fat and cholesterol dissolver that plays an important role in the transmission of nerve impulses. Choline also helps regulate kidney, liver, and gall-bladder functions and aids in the prevention of gallstones.

B12 helps the assimilation of Vitamin A into body tissues by aiding carotene absorption or Vitamin A conversion. It also aids in the production of DNA and RNA, the body's genetic material. B12 needs to be combined with calcium during absorption to benefit the body properly and Nature has provided for that in kefir.

Kefir is rich in thiamin (Vitamin B1), also known as the "morale vitamin" because of its beneficial effects on the nervous system and on mental attitude. Thiamin is linked with enhanced learning capacity, growth in children, and improvement in the muscle tone of the stomach, intestines, and heart. It is essential for stabilizing the appetite and improving digestion, particularly of carbohydrates, sugar, and alcohol.

Kefir from cow's milk is a wonderful source of folate (recommended for pregnant women to prevent fetal spinal deformities). It's vital to the function of methylation and detoxification.

Kefir helps stop food cravings because the body feels nourished as an inner balance is achieved and nutritional deficiencies are corrected.

Kefir provides a "sour" taste. Chinese medicine teaches us there are five tastes necessary for balance in the body; the sour taste is not commonly found in our American diet.

The skin prospers from kefir. It will become moist and creamy and, over time, you will notice a refinement of the pores. You can use kefir externally to help moisturize your skin, but it is beneficial for oily skin too. Fermented milks contain lactic acid, which is one of the naturally occurring alpha hydroxy acids (AHAs) so popular in the cosmetic world today.

Kefir is cooling to the body, so it is ideal to consume when you have a fever or any other condition resulting in body heat such as a herpes outbreak or AIDS. After taking antibiotics, kefir is very useful for reestablishing friendly bacteria in the intestines. Kefir is "Nature's antibiotic."

Easy Milk Kefir from Starter Culture ▪ ▪ ▪ ▪ ▪

Ingredients:

1 quart of milk (cow, goat, or sheep),
    preferably raw

1 sachet of Body Ecology's Kefir Starter

Before you finish drinking your initial batch begin the second by taking out some of the initial batch and combining it with freshly warmed milk (see the table below for ratios). You may repeat this approximately 7 times before you will need another foil packet. Body Ecology's unique kefir starter contains strong, viable bacteria, including lactobacillus bacteria and two strains of beneficial yeast that are unusually hardy, making the transfer process possible.

Directions:

1. Wash a container, preferably glass with an airtight lid.

2. Pour entire foil package of room-temperature Kefir Starter and one quart of milk heated to skin temperature (about 92 degrees) into prepared container.

3. Whisk well and put the lid on the container.

4. Ferment at 72 to 75 degrees for 18 to 24 hours. The kefir will start to thicken, become slightly clumpy, and have a distinct sour aroma.

5. Once thickened, shake or stir vigorously and refrigerate. Kefir will continue to ferment in the refrigerator, but the process is slower.

Food Combining Rules for Drinking Milk Kefir

Kefir is a protein/fat and is easiest to digest when combined with:

- Acidic (sour) fruits, such as strawberries, lemons, limes, grapefruits, pineapples, cranberries, or blueberries
- Raw or lightly steamed vegetables (use as a dip, for example)
- Salads (kefir cheese or in a salad dressing)
- Soaked nuts or seeds and avocados (protein fats)

Milk Kefir Cheese

■ ■ ■ ■ ■

Ingredients:

2 cups milk kefir

Body Ecology's Kefir Starter

Kefir cheese is excellent tossed into salads. It is also delicious flavored (e.g., chopped onions, garlic, sea salt, fresh herbs) and served with an assortment of raw vegetables.

Directions:

1. Make milk kefir (page 182) as instructed, but let the freshly made kefir remain at room temperature for several hours longer. The curds (milk protein) will separate from the whey. The curds will float on top of the whey.

2. Line a strainer with cheesecloth. Place strainer over a bowl and pour the curds and whey mixture into the strainer. The curds will stay in the strainer and the whey will flow through. The whey can be stored in a glass jar in the refrigerator and it makes a delicious addition to a morning smoothie. After removing the whey, refrigerate the strainer and bowl containing the curds and continue to drain for several more hours.

3. Store the cheese curds in a covered container for up to 5 days.

Making More Kefir from the Initial Starter

■ ■ ■ ■ ■

One packet of starter culture will make up to 7 batches of kefir.

Use the amounts in the table below to transfer coconut water or milk from your first batch of kefir to make a second batch. The kefir can be transferred up to 7 times before starting over with a fresh new package of Kefir Starter. A new packet is needed because with each transfer the more aggressive bacteria begin to crowd out the yeast. Your kefir will still be fermented but won't have the beneficial yeast that makes kefir a kefir.

Warmed milk or coconut water	Kefir from previous batch
1 quart	6 tablespoons
½ gallon	2/3 cup
1 gallon	1 cup

These ratios also apply to goat and sheep milk.

Do not add more than recommended amounts from the previous batch. This will result in rapid fermentation and an unpleasantly sour taste.

Notes

Notes

Desserts

The desire for sweet-tasting foods and drinks is quite normal. In fact, our very first food, mother's milk, was warm and sweet and we've formed an emotional bond with this taste, so avoiding sweets is not the answer! But as you know, refined white sugar or corn syrup is poison, and even natural sweeteners like agave and honey will feed yeast and make your body more acidic. Body Ecology recipes use sweeteners like stevia and Lakanto so that you can make sweet treats for you and your family that actually taste like they are made with sugar. Even though traditionally we like to eat desserts after a meal, it's best to eat them separately on an empty stomach. And when you eat them please drink a fermented beverage as well.

Gingery Dairy-Free, Sugar-Free, All-Natural Coconut "Nice Cream" ■ ■ ■ ■ ■ ■

Ingredients:

2 cups fermented coconut meat

2 cups cashews, soaked only 4 hours

4 tablespoons vanilla extract, alcohol-free

¼ cup coconut oil

1 cup filtered water

¼ cup Lakanto

4 drops Body Ecology's stevia liquid concentrate

1½ teaspoons ground ginger

1 teaspoon ground cinnamon

¼ teaspoon ground cloves

1 teaspoon Celtic sea salt

Directions:

1. Purée all ingredients in a blender.

2. Pour into an ice cream maker and freeze according to the manufacturer's instructions.

Have you ever wanted to try your hand at making ice cream but didn't think you had the time? Well, you can make your own ice cream from fermented coconut meat and enjoy it as a dessert or as an addition to a tangy, sweet smoothie. This coconut "nice cream" is delicious and only takes minutes to make...and even less time to disappear from your bowl! It's a delicious treat for spring and summer, and uses all-natural, no-calorie Lakanto sweetener. You may want to double the recipe!

Carrot Dessert Soufflé ■ ■ ■ ■ ■

Ingredients:

1 pound or 2 cups carrots, peeled,
   cut into 3-inch pieces

Filtered water

Pinch of Celtic sea salt

4 tablespoons coconut oil or ghee

3 large eggs

3 tablespoons amaranth or
   buckwheat flour

¼ cup Lakanto

Nutmeg, to taste

1 teaspoon powdered pure vanilla

Directions:

1. Preheat oven to 350 degrees.

2. Using some additional coconut oil or ghee, oil a 6-cup baking dish. Set aside.

3. Place carrots in a saucepan, cover with filtered water, and add a pinch of sea salt. Cook until tender. Drain well and reserve liquid for another use.

4. Purée carrots until smooth. Add remaining ingredients and again purée until smooth. Transfer to the baking dish.

5. Bake 30 to 40 minutes, or until set.

Key Lime Ice Cream ■ ■ ■ ■ ■

Ingredients:

4 to 5 cups coconut kefir cheese (page 178)

3 limes, juiced

½ cup Lakanto

Few drops Body Ecology's stevia liquid
   concentrate, or to taste

⅛ teaspoon pure vanilla extract
   (alcohol-free), or a vanilla bean

Pinch Celtic sea salt

Directions:

1. In a Vitamix or food processor, combine coconut kefir cheese and lime juice, and blend for about 1 minute. Add Lakanto, sea salt, and vanilla. Blend for another 30 seconds.

2. Taste and add stevia, as needed. Pour into freezer-safe container or ice cream maker, and freeze according to the manufacturer's instructions.

If you do not have an ice cream maker, remove your ice cream from the freezer and blend once more just before eating to get the creamiest consistency.

Coconut Vanilla Pudding ■ ■ ■ ■ ■

Ingredients:

1 16 ounce package of coconut meat, thawed,
   or the meat from 3 young coconuts

1 tablespoon vanilla beans

½ cup Lakanto

3 ice cubes

½ cup coconut kefir

Directions:

1. Process all ingredients in a blender until smooth.

2. Scoop into small serving dishes and serve cold.

Key Lime Pudding

■ ■ ■ ■ ■

Ingredients:

½ cup lime juice

1 large avocado, peeled, seeded

½ cup Lakanto

¼ cup plus 2 tablespoons coconut milk or 1 cup coconut kefir cheese (page 178)

2 teaspoons vanilla extract, alcohol-free

¼ teaspoon Celtic sea salt

1 teaspoon Body Ecology's Vitality Super-Green

½ cup + 1 tablespoon coconut oil, measured as a liquid

Directions:

1. Blend all ingredients except coconut oil until smooth. Add coconut oil, and blend thoroughly.

2. Pour into champagne glasses and refrigerate for about an hour, or until firm.

Choose a coconut oil with a neutral flavor from Spectrum or Jarrow. A strong coco-nutty flavor can overpower the delicate sour lime flavor in this recipe. The neutral-flavored oils are more refined than other virgin unrefined oils with a stronger coconut flavor, but their essential fatty acids are stable.

Chocolate Mousse

■ ■ ■ ■ ■

Ingredients:

2 14-ounce cans coconut milk

1 cup Lakanto

½ cup agar flakes

½ cup unsweetened organic dark cocoa powder

2 teaspoons vanilla extract, alcohol-free

1 teaspoon ground cinnamon

¼ teaspoon sea salt

1 tablespoon coconut oil

1 cup walnuts, soaked, chopped

Directions:

1. Combine 2 cans coconut milk, Lakanto, agar flakes, dark cocoa powder, vanilla extract, cinnamon, and sea salt in a saucepan over medium-high heat. Bring to a boil.

2. Reduce the heat to medium-low and simmer for 15 minutes, stirring occasionally.

3. Pour the chocolate mixture into a 2-quart dish and stir in the coconut oil. Let cool at room temperature for 15 minutes. Refrigerate until set.

This delightful mousse is not only delicious, it's dairy-free! As a delicious variation, try adding dried orange peel in step 1.

Lemon Apple Yogurt Parfait

Ingredients:

2 cups of young coconut kefir cheese

1 Granny Smith green apple, cored, peeled, diced

1 teaspoon agar

3 tablespoons Lakanto

½ cup filtered water

1 tablespoon freshly squeezed lemon juice

1 teaspoon lemon zest, finely grated

Few drops Body Ecology's stevia liquid concentrate, or to taste

Mint leaves for garnish

Directions:

1. Make your own coconut kefir (page 176) or coconut kefir cheese (page 178) using Body Ecology Starter cultures.

2. Combine 1 cup of coconut kefir cheese, Granny Smith apple, and a few drops of stevia in a high-speed blender or food processor. Blend until creamy. Move to a mixing bowl.

3. Put the remaining coconut kefir cheese in the blender jar (no need to wash). Add Lakanto, lemon juice, and lemon zest. Blend until creamy. Move to a separate mixing bowl.

4. Boil ½ cup of filtered water. Turn off heat, add agar flakes and stir until dissolved. Quickly add half of the agar gelatin to each bowl and stir. You can re-blend each fruit/cream if you like.

5. Spoon half of the lemon cream into 4 wine glasses then top with half of the green apple cream. Repeat with the remaining lemon and green apple creams. Refrigerate for 20 minutes before serving.

Summer is the perfect time for you to expand on the fruits you eat. Sour fruits like lemons and green apples combine perfectly with the coconut kefir cheese to create a cooling treat so delicious that you won't even know it's sugar-free too.

Remember to eat your fruits in moderation and combine them with fermented foods to enjoy the best results. Sometimes even sour fruits can cause candida to act up. Ideally, fruits should be eaten alone, on an empty stomach. At Body Ecology, we take this a bit further and also suggest eating fruit with a good fermented food or drink. The microflora will eat up the sugar. You can enjoy the delicious flavor and not have to worry about the negative effects.

Quick and Easy Granita

Ingredients:

3 cups filtered water *or* favorite tea

1 ounce cranberry, pomegranate, blueberry,
   or black currant juice concentrate

½ cup Lakanto

Pinch of Celtic sea salt

Directions:

1. Combine, juice concentrate, water, and Lakanto in saucepan. Simmer on low heat for 15 minutes, stirring occasionally.

2. Remove from heat and let cool before pouring into a shallow container. Put into freezer and when the ice has hardened about 95 percent, use the tines of the fork to scrape up shreds of the ice.

3. Return to freezer until ready to eat.

Some juices are more sour than others, so you will have to adjust the amount of sweetener used. Taste the liquid and adjust sweetener accordingly. You can add a few drops of Body Ecology's stevia liquid concentrate to increase the sweet taste. Lakanto and stevia complement each other.

Chocolate Chip Oatmeal Cookies

Ingredients:

1 stick unsalted butter, softened

¾ cup Lakanto

1 teaspoon vanilla extract, alcohol-free

1½ cup amaranth flour (Stage 1) or rice
   flour (Stage 2)

½ teaspoon sea salt

1 teaspoon baking soda

¼ cup boiling water

2 cups gluten-free oats

6 ounces raw cacao nibs

Directions:

1. Preheat oven to 350 degrees.

2. Beat butter, Lakanto, and vanilla extract with a wire whisk until light and fluffy.

3. Add flour and salt and mix well.

4. Dissolve baking soda in boiling water. Add to the mixture.

5. Stir in oats and cacao nibs.

6. Refrigerate for 15 minutes. Use a spoon to drop dough onto cookie sheets, 2 to 3 inches apart.

7. Bake on the middle oven rack for 10 to 15 minutes. Cool on racks. The cookies will be crunchy.

These delicious chocolate chip oatmeal cookies are naturally sweetened with Lakanto, making them sugar-free. They're easy to make and even easier to enjoy! However, flour products of any kind are not healing foods, nor are they healthy for your intestines. Therefore, please consider these Chocolate Chip Oatmeal Cookies a transitional food meant to be eaten only on rare occasions as a special treat. It's best to wait until your inner ecosystem has been well established and healthy. Drinking a few ounces of a probiotic liquid around the same time would be wise.

Triple Berry Sorbet

Ingredients:

1 pint strawberries

1 pint raspberries

1 pint blueberries

1 lemon, juiced

2 cups coconut kefir cheese

½ teaspoon vanilla extract, alcohol-free

Body Ecology's stevia liquid concentrate, to taste

Celtic sea salt, to taste

Directions:

1. Make your own coconut kefir (page 176) or coconut kefir cheese (page 178) using Body Ecology Starter cultures.

2. Blend berries, lemon juice, and vanilla in a high-speed blender. Taste, and add stevia liquid concentrate, as needed. Pour into freezer-safe container or ice cream maker and freeze according to the manufacturer's instructions.

3. Blend the frozen berry mixture with the coconut kefir cheese one more time in the blender then serve.

Strawberry Granita

Ingredients:

2 pounds fresh strawberries, rinsed, hulled

½ cup Lakanto

1 cup filtered water

½ teaspoon fresh squeezed lemon juice

Mint leaves for garnish

Directions:

1. Slice the strawberries and toss them in a large bowl with the Lakanto. Stir until the Lakanto begins to dissolve. Cover and let stand at room temperature for 1 hour, stirring occasionally.

2. Put strawberries, filtered water, and lemon juice in a blender. Purée until smooth. Pour into a shallow container and freeze until solid.

3. Remove pan from freezer and let sit for about 10 minutes. Using a fork, scrape the top of the frozen mixture into icy shreds. Serve in chilled champagne glasses. Garnish with a mint leaf.